QUALITY TEAM LEARNING FOR SCHOOLS

A Principal's Perspective

Also Available from ASQ Quality Press

Improving Student Learning: Applying Deming's Quality Principles in Classrooms
Lee Jenkins

The New Philosophy for K-12 Education: A Deming Framework for Transforming America's Schools
James F. Leonard

Orchestrating Learning With Quality
David P. Langford and Barbara A. Cleary, Ph.D.

Kidgets: And Other Insightful Stories About Quality In Education
Maury Cotter and Daniel Seymour

Total Quality for Schools: A Guide for Implementation
Joseph C. Fields

The Quality Toolbox
Nancy R. Tague

Mapping Work Processes
Dianne Galloway

Team Fitness
Meg Hartzler and Jane E. Henry, Ph.D.

The Change Agents' Handbook: A Survival Guide for Quality Improvement Champions
David W. Hutton

Quality Quotes
Hélio Gomes

To request a complimentary catalog of publications, call 800-248-1946.

QUALITY TEAM LEARNING FOR SCHOOLS
A Principal's Perspective

James E. Abbott, Ph.D.

ASQ Quality Press
Milwaukee, Wisconsin

Quality Team Learning for Schools: A Principal's Perspective
James E. Abbott

Library of Congress Cataloging-in-Publication Data

Abbott, James E., 1945-
    Quality team learning for schools : a principal's perspective /
James E. Abbott.
        p.   cm.
    Includes bibliographical references (p.) and index.
    ISBN 0-87389-384-0 (alk. paper)
    1. Team learning approach in education—United States. 2. School
principals—United States.   I. Title.
LB1032.A23   1998   97-49869
371.39'5—dc21   CIP

© 1998 by ASQ Quality Press

10 9 8 7 6 5 4 3 2 1

ISBN 0-87389-384-0

Acquisitions Editor: Roger Holloway
Project Editor: Roger Holloway

ASQ Mission: To facilitate continuous improvement and increase customer satisfaction by identifying, communicating, and promoting the use of quality principles, concepts, and technologies; and thereby be recognized throughout the world as the leading authority on, and champion for, quality.

Attention: Schools and Corporations
ASQ Quality Press books, audiotapes, videotapes, and software are available at quantity discounts with bulk purchases for business, educational, or instructional use. For information, please contact ASQ Quality Press at 800-248-1946, or write to ASQ Quality Press, P.O. Box 3005, Milwaukee, WI 53201-3005.

For a free copy of the ASQ Quality Press Publications Catalog, including ASQ membership information, call 800-248-1946.

Printed in the United States of America

♾ Printed on acid-free paper

American Society for Quality

ASQ™

Quality Press
611 East Wisconsin Avenue
Milwaukee, Wisconsin 53202

CONTENTS

Education has been under close scrutiny in the United States and throughout the world for the past decade. Disenchantment with the existing American educational system has resulted in a series of national and state reform movements. Reformers have called for strategies to be employed which empower school professionals and parents to determine social and academic needs of students. Other reformers have called for restructuring which has included endeavors to decentralize the management and governance of schools, promote site based decision councils closest to the students, fostered the creation of new roles and responsibilities for all the shareholders in the school culture, and transformed the teaching-learning process.

As agents of change in schools respond to the reform and restructuring movements, it is imperative that they develop new skills and master new approaches to school leadership. No longer are all decisions made by the school administrator alone. Effective schools employ effective team practices.

Quality Team Learning for Schools: A Principal's Perspective, is an excellent book and an important resource for today's school principal and other leaders of change in schools. Developing effective team practice is essential for school leaders of the twenty-first century. Dr. Abbott's book offers a comprehensive balance between theory and strategy. It is a book that provides useful, practical examples and guidance about the topic, delves into the psychological dimensions of team learning and promotes reflective practice. It speaks to the importance of dialogue in teams and how this dialogue can help to reinvent our schools.

Change can be difficult for school leaders. However, learning and applying new leadership tools is essential for the quality results our children deserve. *Quality Team Learning for Schools: A Principal's Perspective*, makes a very important contribution to the literature. It can become a valuable resource for school administrators and shareholders as they pursue their quest for quality and effectiveness in student learning and the ongoing demands of reform.

Beverly H. Neu, Ph.D.
National University

PREFACE

This book encourages educational leaders to send a clear message to fellow educators about the value of team learning in schools.

One of the major underpinnings of this message is the importance of understanding *team psychology*. Little exists in our professional literature about what motivates people to actively participate in team enterprises and the team dynamics that are integrated in team dialogue. Nor is there a legacy of work on the importance of reflective practice.

Team learning is different than team building and teamwork. It is an emerging discipline mandating that we participate in our own learning through building on the learning of others, processing knowledge, self-discovery, and personal reflection. It is less a technological approach and more of a visionary look at the underlying psychology of how people can come together in schools to collaborate effectively.

This vision will lead schoolpeople—all the shareholders in the school community ranging from parents to teacher assistants—to ask themselves some primary questions about how to get the school on the right track toward quality. Is the school committed to developing the employees and parents? Are there open lines of communication? Is there a high level of trust in the culture? Are teams established to focus their energy and resources to address important projects and themes?

It is fundamentally impractical for school principals to confront the prevailing issues of school life competently by themselves. They need to employ all the human resources available if they are to have any hope of establishing direction for improvement of teaching and learning within the school walls. The more people involved in balanced dialogue about school improvement practices, the greater the possibility for meaningful change. These schoolpeople—parents, teachers, support staff, administrators, and students—ought to have true ownership of the school. A school does not belong only to a school district, it belongs to all the shareholders also.

There is a unique wisdom that exists in teams that carefully unfolds as people engage in a trusting forum that celebrates and recognizes the importance of the individual. Their collective interaction encourages the mining of the untapped talent of colleagues as they define and redefine projects, practices, and organizational operations.

Team learning is a beginning place for learning opportunities in the workplace. To labor together is a natural state for mankind. To strive together for the mutual benefit of children in schools is noble. Team learning underscores the possibilities that exist for schoolpeople to collaborate together and to communicate for effective understanding so they can make important change happen in their schools.

This book is written in a nonpedantic style. There are a number of titles available that deal with team building and how to maximize teamwork by presenting a mechanical, "by the numbers" approach, and while they are helpful in training individuals on the technical aspects of team building, these books gloss over team learning, if they mention it at all. Consequently, they fail to present the dynamic, human side that takes place in vital *learning* for individuals and their teammates. This is meant to be a book about self-discovery and reflective practice that promises to lead to important change.

As learners, we have to reflect on our practice regarding teaching and learning. When we learn about ourselves and how we affect the larger organization, we develop the capacity to ask primary questions about processes in our schools and how we can work together to improve them. As we continue on our personal learning curves, we understand that we need to listen to others, engage them in meaningful dialogue and that we ought to *slow down*. We can accomplish so much more in our schools when we work together.

There are 80,000 schools in our nation. Quality practices have had only minuscule impact on them because existing books relate sanctimonious approaches with charts and multiple lists of "how to's." Team learning is part of an emerging "soft issue revolution" in our schools. As every educator knows, learning is a personal, human experience. It doesn't flow by the numbers and it doesn't adhere to specific rules. It involves people collaboratively learning from one another and with one another to affect change.

By relating my "hands-on" experiences in the following chapters, I hope to shed some light on the emerging discipline of team learning.

ACKNOWLEDGEMENTS

A book is never the product of a single person. I am indebted to my wife, Teri, and daughter, Stephanie, as well as my entire family for their patience and support from the time I wrote the initial manuscript, through the subsequent rewrites. They, above all, have been vital links to my lifelong learning journey.

Many academic faculties across the nation have given invaluable assistance in the writing of this book, some more than they realize. Many offered thoughtful suggestions and warm encouragement which sustained and buoyed me so that I could go to a higher place on my personal learning curve. At Harvard, Roland Barth has served as a role model and mentor-coach for my modest writing. He expressed an unfailing belief in me, from the onset, to share my *craft knowledge*. Likewise, Richard Ackerman, Gordy Donaldson, Joe Richards, Jan Arend Brands, Carol Wilson, Don Hoecherl, Larry Feldman and Gayle Moeller from the Harvard University International Network of Principal's Centers have played a variety of roles supporting the vision for this book. A special debt is also owed to Beverly Neu of National University for her special contribution. At UCLA, Rae Jean Williams and JoAnn Isken were important allies, encouraging me to venture my spoken thoughts to the printed page.

I am grateful to colleagues in the Los Angeles Unified School District who, over the years, have inspired me to continue writing articles and books: Stu Bersnstein, Carol Ogawa, Sam Marchese, Roberta Burk, Jim Burk and Gabe Cortina have validated my attempts at reinventing schools while attempting to accomplish the same mission.

In addition, I must recognize Kelley Cardinal, acquisitions editor, Lynn Steines, project editor, and Jan Hoff, my personal editor for transforming undecipherable sentences into ones that flow. For me, no acknowledgement section would be complete without honoring March Laree Jacques for her sustained interest in my writings and her search for quality. Lastly, I want to express my sincere appreciation to Roger Holloway, Manager of ASQ Quality Press, for his encouragement and direction in bringing this project to publication. His creative participation in the multiple planning and operational activities so essential for my book's successful completion, made the dream a reality.

James E. Abbott, Ph.D.
Redondo Beach, California

CHAPTER

Team Psychology

Schools are told not to do anything different and then graded on originality.

—Anonymous

The business world abounds with organizations that have reaped the benefits of the quality movement and experienced the rich promise of transformational change. We in the field of education also need to examine the possibilities for creating a capacity in our schools for profound change. The critical question for educators is: Where do we begin the process? One approach is to build upon a strength that lives at each school. Which is to say, we need to build upon the existing talents in our school culture. Building dynamic teams and the crucial prospect of generating team learning go to the center of creating the process that will broker collective talents to create the successful schools of the future.

Much of the criticism of the schools in our contemporary society is unwarranted. In reality, we are doing about as well as we always have in this century. The difference is that we are doing it with a needier, poorer, more transient, and more diverse student population than in the past. Public schools have had to take on the extra burden of fostering the ethical and social development of students because families and communities are more fragmented than they have been in the past, but students still require preparation for the demands of the workplace and for active participation in our democratic society.

In fact, schools need to accomplish much more than ever in our history. We want our schools both to educate a "higher proportion of students to much higher levels of cognitive accomplishment and capacity"[1]

1

due to increased demands in the workplace, and to prepare these students for the social rigors of the next century.

The promise of quality management principles and practices and the archetypes of systems thinking are only beginning to surface in visionary models in the world of education. The purpose of this text is to advance an important aspect of the systems thinking movement as applied to schools—that of team learning.

Teams may appear to be easy to assemble because we all have had the experience of being involved in schoolyard athletics to draw upon when reflecting on teamwork. However, the intellectual pursuit of teams is very different from the physical. Peter Senge, author of *The Fifth Discipline: The Art and Practice of the Learning Organization*, states that the prospect of *team learning* is the most difficult of his five disciplines to master.[2]

Two of the linchpins of the quality movement are "continuous improvement" and "constancy of purpose." Continuous improvement involves the collecting of valuable data and transferring the data into strategies that can be measured for effectiveness. Many outstanding books, on themes ranging from statistical process control to strategic planning, cover this territory.

Constancy of purpose, on the other hand, involves high levels of employee involvement that promote avenues in the organization for purposeful dialogue and reflection. Constancy of purpose is about keeping the passion alive. Team learning is part of this aspect of a quality enterprise. While studying data focuses on little things to be measured, the dialogue promoted in team learning brings little things into focus.

Schools are not just about data, such as test scores or attendance rates. Schools are also about humanity, commitment, and learning. It is team learning that drives action and creates real change. Teams can continuously invent new information and learning as ideas grow in energy fields between people. Individuals, on teams, can move forward by generating learning that encourages them to anticipate what they need to learn.

Team learning challenges each player to reach new levels of personal and professional effectiveness. Effective teams alter our understanding of how a group of people can work together to communicate their personal visions to a point at which they recognize a common, underlying purpose. From this purpose, a shared vision flows that demands that each team member tap his or her personal talents to fulfill the goals of the team as well as to achieve organizational objectives.

The wisdom of teams is an evolutionary process. Teams achieve enlightenment as a result of operating under an umbrella of support and trust from the leadership at the school. They acquire an intelligence by participating in meaningful dialogue opportunities and having the occasion to reflect upon the learning process. There is a sensibility and sensitivity that permeates effective teams. In addition, they tend to be unfailingly intelligent.

An emerging view of psychologists and biologists in the nineties is that groups of people who collaborate together can maximize opportunities for team learning in work situations. Critics of team collaborations have long asserted that team members change their composition too much and too often to nurture a consistency that evokes meaningful change. However, David Sloan Wilson of the State University of New York believes that an ensemble of people, working in teams, can create a united vision of organizational quality and produce quality results—even if the team assembles intermittently and if some of its members depart or enter at various times. Dr. Wilson has found that "organized groups may have cognitive properties that differ from those of the individuals who constitute the group." The amalgamation of talents within the group can create strategies, goals, and results over and above the individual special skills of people who compose the team. In addition, Wilson found that many team members are willing to work longer hours and take on more assignments in order to achieve desired results.[3]

Team learning develops over time, building on short-term results and a compelling desire by team members to accomplish breakthrough projects.

Higher-performance teams can be replicated in any school. But they must be allowed to be self-directed and to receive stewardship from the school leadership to flourish. Those schools interested in promoting organizational change ought to have many teams engaged in transferring knowledge and information on a number of levels. Effective teams can be models for other teams at a school. As long as meaningful dialogue is modeled in the team enterprise, teams will learn to maximize group enlightenment that supports creativity and profound organizational learning.

Teams have a way of bringing out the best in others. They stimulate opportunities for self- and organizational discovery. Superior teams have an ability to release the immense power of human ingenuity. They create the possible where the impossible existed before. Teams can make transformational thinking a reality and provide forums whereby their members may embark on an extraordinary journey toward self-reflective discovery.

TEAM DYNAMICS

The most effectual teams are created in a trusting, nonthreatening environment. For innovation to prosper, leadership has to assume the lead in framing a team enterprise by creating assurances that open communication will be expected. Principals or other team leaders at the school will have to abandon some of their most fundamental assumptions about school district hierarchy, as well as their own imposed lines of authority, at the site in this new model. Developing self-organizing and self-directing teams at a school flies in the face of the core principles of bureaucracy. We must take seriously Dr. W. Edwards Deming's challenge that 85 percent of the responsibility for quality in any organization rests with management. Therefore, as a group, superintendents, principals, and school boards must commit to the stewardship of quality enterprises in schools for meaningful change to happen. Schools are the last major organizational model in America, if you discount the vast federal government, to operate in a bygone bureaucratic model paradigm. It is up to the individuals in leadership roles in school districts to heed the winds of change in a contemporary society. Quality schools will happen when schoolpeople are tapped as valued resources.

It takes a special kind of leader to frame dynamic team models at a school. Team building, much like leadership, is an art form. Not everyone can do it. Even those with the enthusiasm to attempt to accelerate change in schools will be hard-pressed to accomplish such an undertaking without a strong personal vision for success. But the stakes remain far too high. Our children are much too important for schools to continue to squander opportunities for bold change that can translate to improved academic achievement.

Some of the major components of a productive working partnership are suggested below. As you read them, remember that they are part of an underlying framework for action.

♦ **Flexibility:** There should be no set structure, or a very limited structure design, for teams so that they can best utilize the diverse skills, personalities, and talents of the participants.

♦ **Shared knowledge:** A networked learning process is the goal of a learning organization. Teams are required to interact and share information and knowledge with other teams to optimize their productivity. In turn, they must be able to access information from a variety of sources within the organization to achieve their goals.

♦ **Working smarter:** Team learning enhances working styles and creates a culture wherein people do not have to work harder to accomplish valued results, because they are working smarter in high-leverage teams.

Schools are a place where a number of people such as teachers, support staff, parents, students, and the principal have all gathered as a result of unrelated circumstances. But the fact that they are all together by hap-

> ## LEARNING WINDOW 1.1
> ### Collaborative Skills for Teams
>
> ✔ **Defining** = Dialogue within the group to share knowledge.
> ✔ **Analyzing** = Examine issues in context of the goals of the team.
> ✔ **Synthesizing** = Build a common reality by inviting input.
>
> Adapted from Bensimon and Neuman

penstance should not diminish their capacity to form group interactions and learning. Similarly, teams are composed of schoolpeople who may not have naturally converged together. It is the challenge of the leadership of the school to maximize the learning potential of the team by framing their goals and, in some cases, assisting with the selection of some team players to make sure the right people are in place to leverage for positive results.

Every person in the school culture wants to make a contribution. Many desire to assume leadership roles. Some are compelled by a yearning to achieve results. Others are driven to participate to be recognized. One of the unalloyed benefits of team building is that these opportunities lead some individuals who normally do not aspire to assume leadership roles to volunteer to head important team enterprises and to try still other new and bold experiences.

W. Edwards Deming made a landmark contribution to the cause of organization learning by researching the basic psychological needs of workers. Dr. Deming felt that work should hold such high intrinsic value that it would intertwine with the very fiber of life. This is the essence of the concept he introduced: "profound knowledge."

Profound knowledge, according to Deming, has subsystem components that are so inexorably interwoven that they become inseparable. To completely understand it is to commit to the whole notion. These subsystems of knowledge are

- ♦ Appreciation for a system
- ♦ Theory of variation
- ♦ Theory of knowledge
- ♦ Psychology[4]

Since the thrust of this book is on how teams learn, it is not necessary to delve into all of Deming's subsystems. But an exploration of "psychology" is essential to a thorough understanding of the complexity of how teams work together.

Psychology, for Deming, is the most powerful component of the four subsystems of profound knowledge. He believed that all people have an innate inclination to learn and be innovative. Deming felt that engaging in work could recapture, for adults, their lost penchant for learning and inquiry. He thought work experiences could be valued and applied to real life. Deming surmised that work should offer a unique opportunity for personal and professional growth.

Dr. Deming's emphasis on the psychology of the individual runs through the core of this book. Team learning explores the underlying psychology of individuals. It is less technical than philosophical. The value Deming afforded the psychology of profound knowledge sets him aside from all other total quality management (TQM) experts. It is the study of psychology that makes him a philosopher as well as an expert practitioner of quality.

ORGANIZATIONAL CHANGE

In productive team models, contributions from team players are the embers that keep the fire of creativity alive and self renewing. In effective teams, it is not one's title or rank of succession in the school hierarchy that is important. It is viable ideas that are the marketable commodity. Those individuals who offer the best ideas are the ones who are listened to in the culture, regardless of their rank in the organizational structure.

Teams are a straightforward opportunity for tapping the psychological capacity of each person to be encouraged to pursue the possibilities of optimization of talent, ensure high levels of participation, and promote risk taking. Teams are from the new age school model of teaching people how to fish rather than the archaic school model of feeding them and keeping them dependent and passive.

We seldom scrutinize the effectiveness of the total institutional and organizational subsystem in schools. By not understanding the importance of structuring and supporting effective lines of communication and the value of team learning, we set ourselves up for failure.

Peter Drucker has indicated that schools are far too concerned about rules and regulations, when they should be focused on performance and results.[5] It is time for us to revisit our product—student achievement—and place it in the context of how youngsters will be able to use their academic preparation in the workplace.

Senge believes that when enough people come together to share a vision of implementing desired change, they galvanize to become a "learning organization" that encourages people to fully integrate their talents and skills for the greater prosperity of the organization.[6] All employees utilize their utmost talents in such a culture. The leaders of a learning organization become so thoroughly engaged in defining their vision and becoming the architects of a learning community that they come to feel they are "part of a larger purpose that goes beyond their organization."[7]

LEADERS

Leaders not only have personal visions of the future, they push for others to have their own visions. They understand the desire within everyone to express beliefs and notions about the possibilities of a new culture. They live and breathe profound knowledge. They are committed to a shared vision that unites everyone with a common purpose.

These leaders encourage employees in the workplace to see relationships and processes holistically. These people are advocates for moving "beyond blame" and avoiding symptomatic solutions that provide only temporary resolution of problems and fail to address "underlying causes." They promote "stewardship" of the new culture[8] and urge worker passion in a quest for quality.

There are educational leaders who are dissatisfied with their product and realize that there has to be a better approach to marshaling improvement in student achievement. These are the inspirational, sometimes revolutionary, leaders who envision the possibilities for TQM and learning organizations. They see the value of bringing people together to think in nontraditional, nonlinear fashions. It will be nontraditional thinking that will inspire the changes required of schools.

In *The Fourth Instinct: The Call of the Soul*, Arianna Huffington traces our human condition through four stages of development. The fourth stage, *personal fulfillment*, happens when one is able to identify and collaborate with others in meaningful, interactive relationships. Huffington believes there is an intuitive desire within the human spirit to identify with others and bond in relationships that have a common purpose.[9] This type of relationship has applications to the world of work.

LEARNING WINDOW 1.2

"Most managers get into trouble because they forget to think in circles."

—*Karl Weick*

Functioning in a collaborative work team that has quality as its centerpiece is a logical forum in which to achieve this desire for meaningful collaboration. The intuitive leader who arms himself or herself with the tools of a positive philosophy of life, guided by ethics and sustained by perseverance, will come to comprehend a deeper meaning for life as outlined by the dimensions established by the fourth instinct. This person is a risk taker who can extol the virtues of daring to try new and innovative approaches within the work culture. Leaders value learning. For them, learning has no beginning and no end. It is an unbroken circle that invites human collaboration.

Searching for truth from within encourages leaders to assume the trailblazing life of a role model. By becoming a lifelong learner, the leader advocates the commendability of ongoing learning for all. A "deliverance" of sorts is the end result of fostering lifelong education. By becoming actively engaged in all aspects of life, one can become a better person and more productive at work.

PEOPLE IN TEAMS

Teams, in and of themselves, do not ensure a quality commitment to the customer. Peter Scholtes, a senior consultant with Joiner Associates of Madison, Wisconsin, says, "Teamwork is not enough." To his way of thinking, teamwork must be accompanied by an intensive focus on customer satisfaction and operational improvements.[10] Jon Katzenbach and Douglas Smith, in their book, *The Wisdom of Teams*, argue that teams with a superior performance track record tend to accomplish this degree of competency, not based on catchy team-building exercises, which corporations and school districts seem to be so fond of, but by adhering to a strong commitment to fulfill performance challenges.[11] Successful models of change produce a desire in the team to relish future projects for change.

LEARNING WINDOW 1.3

"Communities of learners seem to be committed above all to discovering conditions that elicit and support human learning."

—*Roland Barth*

There are many individuals who have written outstanding essays and books about teams and quality circles. How teams overcome internal conflict, encourage risk taking, respond to the changing needs of their members and reach consensus are dynamics that each must withstand and overcome. Nonetheless, successful teams will always be grounded with a focus on meeting customer needs and always hold a proper regard for the "people" who make up the organization. The characteristics of the team will, in most cases, be dependent upon the sagacious vision and trustworthiness of individuals who emerge as the leaders of the teams and the people who comprise them. Teams and quality circles are an important aspect of any work culture. However, it is the people who make up these teams who become the driving force for effective, systemic, and lasting change. Leaders of teams are truly important, but the source of wisdom in teams rests with the entire membership. The best teams emphasize the holistic nature of the dialogue enterprise between themselves and their customers.

The people in the organization address customer needs. For school districts interested in improving student achievement, their leverage in addressing customer requirements rests with the people who constitute the organization. Regardless of the amount of money invested in technology, research, and marketing, the edge a business or school district has on its competition rests with the individuals who work for it and how much information and discretion they have to make the best possible decisions regarding daily issues. There are no secrets here—people make all the difference in the world.

Dissatisfaction with the present system is a key element in creating a climate for change. Employees may not have a proper awareness level of their failure to meet customer expectations unless they have a complete understanding of who their customers are. Employees of a school system can come to understand that student achievement is everyone's business through team dialogue opportunities. If student achievement is not meeting customer satisfaction levels, then people in the school system have a civic duty to explore the possibilities of changing processes that have caused this disfavorable situation.

In our nation's history, it has been the lot of educators and other employees of school districts to attempt to maintain the status quo of an anachronistic system that was originally designed to teach youngsters *how to work in factories*. Many educators fail to realize that school institutions are fundamentally "out of sync" with the demands of our modern society.

Schoolpeople who can make connections with others in open dialogue forums about improving teaching and learning can use their intrinsic motivation to create a climate for change. When profound knowledge is added to the mix of any culture, change is inevitable.

MY INTRODUCTION TO COMMITTEES

I recall being invited, at a point early in my career as a principal, to serve on a Superintendent's Select Committee to uncover the core issues of why there was so little parent involvement in our schools. I had been a principal for only a few years and remember feeling very good about being invited to join with other principals and assistant superintendents—some of the elite minds of the Los Angeles Unified School District—to address this important topic.

At the conclusion of the initial meeting, our facilitator gave all of us a "homework" assignment—to do research on practical applications to improve parent involvement. We were scheduled to reconvene in two weeks to share with our fellow committee members our findings.

I jumped at the opportunity to do the research and returned to the next meeting with materials to distribute to each member. The meeting went on for two hours. The facilitator never asked for the homework reports. Near the conclusion of the meeting I asked for an opportunity to share my research. I passed out my meticulously researched packets, spoke briefly, and asked for committee members to give me input.

Needless to say, each of them—seasoned committee member veterans that they were—stared at me in total disbelief. None of them had done any homework and they didn't plan on doing any. The facilitator pushed for closure, declaring that all the items discussed in the agendaless meeting would be promptly passed along to the superintendent for action.

It was at this juncture that I realized that this was a "committee." They weren't supposed to accomplish anything—they were a committee. They knew their role and their purpose very well. I was completely "out of step" with the program.

I have refused to serve on any "committees" in my subsequent fifteen years with the district. Whenever I have been asked to serve, I politely beg off. I do not have time to do committee work. I want to work with teams. I want to work in a learning enterprise that can prompt action and change. I want to engage in personal and team dialogue to promote learning. Hence, my passion for teams, team building, and team learning. It is in these engagements that transformation becomes a possibility.

LEADERS OF CHANGE

The emergence of the importance of soft issues is a recent phenomenon for schools. Leaders in schools have the responsibility of devising frameworks at their sites so that they can unleash the intrinsic desires schoolpeople have to improve their work culture. It is up to the leaders of schools to make certain that avenues exist for people to speak freely about their insights on issues and that an audience is available to give feedback so that professional development, personal growth, and improved processes are initiated.

One such process that we have employed with excellent results in encouraging schoolpeople to take control of their professional development and personal growth has been my "Desperado Team." I have used this confederation at the last three schools where I have served as principal, with unwavering success. The Desperado Team meets periodically, as an ad hoc group, consisting of teachers, support staff, parents, and myself—with no prescribed agenda. The purpose of each meeting is for the associates of the team to identify an issue and work together to solve it.

The problem may concern instructional delivery, discipline, or safety. It is usually an issue that is not a topic in normal interactions at the school, such as faculty or grade level meetings, yet requires serious attention and open dialogue. Desperado Team members view themselves as resources to solve these issues.

I have found that there are always individuals at a school who are willing to participate in self-directed teams that tackle difficult issues. As a principal, I have determined that it is my responsibility to invite them to dialogue about how to solve those issues by creating a framework for them to speak about improving practices and processes and creating meaningful change. This framework must be invitational, not institutional. The result is our Desperado Team.

The way I initiated the team may well be replicated by other school administrators. As a newly assigned principal at my current school, I wrote a notice in the weekly bulletin early in the school year: School leaders meet Tuesday at 7:30 A.M. in the school library.

Now, it is important to note that we have a large number of leadership councils at our school that include parents, support staff, and teachers as members. There are leadership councils, school site councils, grade level teams, and other such groups; therefore several people in the school were confused as to whether they should attend. When I wrote "school leaders" they were unsure if I was addressing them as members of various councils.

Consequently at 7:30 A.M. on Tuesday morning when I walked into the library I had a large group of people in the audience. I remember sitting down and welcoming everyone, at which time one teacher asked, "Jim, I'm not sure if I'm supposed to be at this meeting. I'm an elected representative to the School Site Council. Is this a meeting for us?" Others in the assembledge were nodding their heads as if in agreement.

I responded, "Yes. If you consider yourself to be a leader at the school, I want you here." I went on to indicate that it would be my fervent hope that all who came to this initial meeting uncertain if they were required to attend would attend future meetings because they desired to be part of the change process in our school.

I went on to tell them that I know that there are many leaders at a school and that it is important for me to be able to tap into their existing talents to help me make the quality improvements that would be required. I needed everyone on this team to work together to identify problems or express visionary ideas, develop strategies, and shepherd projects through to their fruition. Their purpose was to engage in dialogue about what variety of activities needed to be performed, what resources were required, and what subteams were required to make their goals become reality.

LEARNING WINDOW 1.4

Stem Questions for Your Own Desperado Team

1. What aspects of school life would you like to change?
2. How can communication at our school improve?
3. How will the opportunity to dialogue in teams change you?

I wanted people who were desperate to have the opportunity to contribute solutions and create initiatives for the improvement of school life. By tapping into their intrinsic desires for meaningful change, I was ensuring that I had a team of committed people who knew what the problems were firsthand. The Desperadoes were encouraged to present issues and play a major role in their solution. Their intrinsic desire to create meaningful change was validated in the framework of the Desperado organization, and striking results ensued.

Among the major changes that happened in the first year included: attendance incentives were created to improve student and teacher attendance; three major standing teams (Instruction, Budget/Public Relations, School-wide Governance) were formed to act on issues related to their domains; Extended Conversation Teams were organized; an Alternative Performance Evaluation was designed and put into practice; portfolios and rubrics became a part of each teacher's evaluation arsenal; grants for technology were written as well as funded; and open access to the school categorical budget was enacted upon.

Leadership is important in transforming the intrinsic desires people have to improve their school into action. When leaders have a proper understanding of team psychology, they can create a framework for people to learn and continue learning from one another. People engaged in team learning will assume the ethical responsibility to lead change. By working collaboratively to share their desires for a better school, teams like the Desperadoes were encouraged to collectively develop powerful processes to achieve quality in our school.

Team learning is an exponent of team psychology. Team psychology is tapped by inviting everyone to participate in dialogue about creating and defining performance conditions and improved teaching and learning processes. Team learning occurs when people pull together to share their knowledge to develop specific strategies for change that are aligned with the mission of the organization.

ENDNOTES

1. Eric Schaps, "Pushing Back for the Center," *Education Week*, January 22, 1997.
2. Peter Senge, *The Fifth Discipline: The Art and Practice of the Learning Organization* (New York: Doubleday, 1990).

3. David Sloan Wilson. "Return of the Group," *Science News* 148 (November 1995).

4. W. Edwards Deming, *Out of the Crisis* (Cambridge, MA: M.I.T. Center for Advanced Engineering Study, 1986).

5. Peter Drucker, *Managing the Non-Profit Organization* (New York: HarperCollins, 1990).

6. Peter Senge, *The Fifth Discipline: The Art and Practice of the Learning Organization* (New York: Doubleday, 1990).

7. Charles Watson, *Managing with Integrity: Insights from America's C.E.O.'s* (New York: Praeger, 1991).

8. Mary Walton, *The Deming Management Method* (New York: Perigree Books, 1986).

9. Arianna Huffington, *The Fourth Instinct: The Call of the Soul* (New York: Simon & Schuster, 1994).

10. Bradford McKee, "Turn Your Workers into a Team," *Nations Business*, July 1992.

11. Jon R. Katzenbach, and Douglas K. Smith, *The Wisdom of Teams: Creating a High Performance Organization* (Cambridge, MA: Harvard Business School Press, 1993).

LEARNING WINDOWS

1.1 E.M. Bensimon, and A. Neuman, *Redesigning Collegiate Leadership: Teams and Teamwork in Higher Education* (Baltimore: Johns Hopkins University Press, 1993).

1.2 Karl Weick, *The Social Psychology of Organizing* (Reading, MA: Addison-Wesley Publishers, 1979).

1.3 Roland Barth, *Improving Schools from Within: Teachers, Parents and Principals Can Make the Difference* (San Francisco: Jossey-Bass, 1991).

CHAPTER

Team Communication

"We ourselves, and with each other by our converse, can create not an architecture of global scope, but an immense, intricate network of intimacy, illumination, and understanding."

—J. Robert Oppenheimer, as quoted by Gerald Holton in Daedalus, *Fall 1977*

The primary modality in which teams learn is by speaking with one another. However, it would be a mistake to assume that, just because people in the team are talking, they are communicating.

Effective teams communicate effectively. In the team setting, the means of communication is through language, the language being constructed in meaningful dialogue sessions. Interaction within the team is productive when interpersonal communication is effective.

It all sounds too easy. Yet good team communication is one of the most difficult processes to master. In this chapter we will explore why schoolpeople come together to join in team enterprises and how effective communication keeps them together in a sustained collaboration to improve processes and produce valued projects for the benefit of the school culture.

School transformation can take place only when all the players that compose the shareholders of the school have an opportunity to voice their concerns, ideas, hopes, and aspirations. Sometimes, this expression becomes memorialized in a vision or mission statement. However, real transformational change is best accomplished in the daily activities of high-performance teams that are focused on accomplishing goals that are aligned to the school mission.

LEARNING WINDOW 2.1

"Some managers think that just because they are speaking, that they are communicating."

—*Dogbert (Scott Adams)*

The quality of the communication that takes place within a team has direct correlation with the quality of the eventual product or outcome generated by the team. Effective communication is a valuable currency. Conversations explore the "whys," "hows," and "what's next" that ought to be addressed.

Schools are not the easiest cultures to change. Most school districts are highly structured, top-down organizations, burdened with volumes of education codes and board policies that inhibit change rather than encourage it. Consequently, schools have become the last broad-scale entity in America to realize the advantages inherent in implementing Total Quality Management or learning organization disciplines.

This does not mean that there are not many well-intentioned individuals who work in school districts. The commitment and character of these dedicated people goes without question. Young people owe them a debt of gratitude for their perseverance and professionalism. The best educators, support staffs, principals, superintendents, and school board members find ways to rise above the bureaucracy to make schools a meaningful place for educational processes to flourish.

However, the system in which these dedicated people work needs a major retrofitting so they can become more customer oriented. Team learning groups can encourage dialogue and collaboration, so people have a forum to explore their own ideas and passions about how to improve schools.

Teams afford schoolpeople an opportunity to join in chorus with others to take up the cause of inventing quality schools. When given the chance to create a vision of the possible, they can move away from the bankrupt vision of the past. Effective teams learn to recognize the efficacy of challenging each other to reach a little bit higher than they have in the past. They encourage trust, self-motivation, evolvement, and the belief that individuals have some control over their immediate environment.

Evolvement is the product of effective communication practices within teams. Schools have not had a history of successful experiences with teams. Most of the communication that has occurred in the past is limited to faculty meetings, committee work, and limited interfacing between teachers during recess and lunch breaks. Therefore, schoolpeople have not had meaningful occasions to engage in quality dialogue about how to improve learning conditions, student life, academic preparation, professional development, or student achievement. Limited opportunities for interfacing have much to do with how isolated teachers are from teacher colleagues on the same campus, and even from parents.

Consequently, schoolpeople have tended to settle for a semipermanent estrangement within the schoolyard walls rather than attempt to communicate about their hopes and aspirations. Opening avenues of communication within the school tells us that human life should be a statement about living. When people express their opinions on important issues about school life they help to keep the agenda of schools aligned with the vision.

Through a balance of advocacy and inquiry, team members can approach school issues and projects as both teachers and learners. As advocates of change, they learn to rely upon each other and dramatically bond. When team players communicate about important issues, they quickly come to realize that the best resource for the solution of any problem lies within the talents of the people who know the most about the problem. Therefore, the individuals who have the most expertise and information about issues need to be invited into the circle to dialogue about how to best resolve the pressing concerns that confront schools today.

In private industry, teams are routinely composed of individuals who possess crucial skills and talents that are applicable to the project or issue at hand. The world of business understands the importance of soliciting the best talent to get the highest quality results. Schools would like to do this but, because teachers work in isolated spheres, no one is really sure who has expertise to offer on given topics. In addition, there is such limited information about the talents of parents and resources offered by businesses in the outlying community, that they tend to be omitted, out of hand, from consideration.

The ceiling of expectations rests with the vision of the school leadership. School administrators are not trained in university course work in examining the contemporary horizons of their communities with an eye on valuing input from a variety of sources.

```
┌─────────────────────────────────────────────────────┐
│                 LEARNING WINDOW 2.2                   │
│                  The Team Advantage                   │
│                                                       │
│  ✔ Creates a trusting environment.                    │
│  ✔ Improves morale.                                   │
│  ✔ Generates greater buy-in on processes and plans.   │
│  ✔ Values and uses diverse talents and viewpoints.    │
│  ✔ Improves work relationships and reduces isolationism. │
│  ✔ Team members gain a broader view of factors affecting │
│    school life.                                       │
│  ✔ Promotes creativity.                               │
│  ✔ Increases quality of student achievement.          │
│                                                       │
```

PSYCHOLOGICAL CAPACITIES OF A TEAM

There is an ever-expanding benefit of having productive teams in schools. They are all extensions of basic quality management behaviors that contribute to the development of people in the school culture.

When decision making is extended to teams, the people who comprise those teams respond by increasing their willingness to risk and stretch. Individuals who might try to sabotage team efforts can't get a foothold when everyone on the team is charged with a responsibility to become a developer of ideas, coach others, and establish high performance goals.

With the involvement of schoolpeople who have never before been asked to work as a group on solving problems or developing a process, something special happens. When successful teams develop their own goals, establish their own feedback mechanisms, and are charged with shaping the framework for a course of action, there is little room for saboteurs to make a negative impact. The energy of the team, supported by peer pressure, tends to discount even the most discouraging person from steering a team off course. This is because the best teams don't only work as a team, they learn to behave as a team, unified by their collective vision and passion to achieve unparalleled quality as an outcome of their collaboration.

Although there may be attempts to create district-wide quality management practices, the school must be the primary unit of change. Teams comprised of schoolpeople can work together to tighten, clarify, and focus

---

LEARNING WINDOW 2.3
Adult Learning in Team Dialogue

✔ Most adults learn best in small groups.
✔ Adults can learn from a wide range of interests.
✔ Adults are more positive about their learning experience when they feel some sense of control over directing the project at hand.
✔ Adults are self-directed learners, gravitating toward intrinsic motivation.

---

on orchestrating paths to improve teaching and learning practices. Significant improvements in teaching and learning have a beginning point in effective team dialogue.

Schoolpeople must express a strong desire to want to improve upon current practices. They must also come to embrace the enormous possibilities that rest with their intrinsic desires to improve processes. If school teams are not included by the school administrators in meaningful processes, schools will be just going through the motions of talking about change.

A basic precept of adult learning is based on the fact that adults will commit to involvement in processes that they perceive to be pertinent to their personal and professional growth. The content of the dialogue creating team dynamics is one that is a perfect fit for adult learning and retention. When contributions and learning are emphasized in the context of team dialogue, people come to feel they are part of a concrete, direct experience that affects their learning.

Part of the dialogue experience serves to meet another need for adult learning—that adults need feedback. Conversations offer immediate feedback by peers, a facilitator, or a group of colearners who comprise the team. Team dialogue sessions offer many opportunities for feedback while refining the processes, creating opportunities, and advancing team-created goals.

Cognitive learning moves beyond basic understanding toward the realm of application, analysis, synthesis, and outcomes in good team exchanges. When team members share, analyze, and reflect on their new learning, they become educated about how different players on the team contribute to the whole effort.

Adults will work well in teams when they are focused on common goals and share a common destiny. In the best teams, everyone assumes responsibility for achieving team goals. When schoolpeople experience the elation of working with others in tapping resources, thinking strategically, and improving processes, problem solving can come to be viewed as an enabling event.

WORKING ON THE SELF CYCLE

Robert M. Pirsig's *Zen and the Art of Motorcycle Maintenance* is a provocative book that invites the reader to journey with the author on a trip across the road maps of the human mind. One of the premises of the book is that the "cycle" everyone is in need of working on is the cycle we call ourselves.[1] Conversations offer an intriguing invitation for each of us to explore an ever evolving landscape of human interaction. And while we can come to view the team players as rapt repositories of wisdom, it is our learning that is the most valued aspect of the experience. When we give voice to the conversation, we grow bit by bit.

Hence, from a selfish point of view, team dialogue is a beacon of self-help. The substance of the exchange offers something special for each of us that can be both affecting and instructive. We hear the insights of others to broaden our whole field of experience. Conversations and learning are intimate companies. They are inseparable partners in helping us discover new places in our heads and hearts.

Although business school libraries abound with authors who extol the virtues of team networks, team building, and synergy, schools are very different places. Teachers tend to work in isolation from other teachers. Bell schedules dictate recess and lunch breaks so that the entire faculty seldom meets together. When teachers do meet together, it is in faculty meetings where they are "talked to" rather than "talked with" by the school principal. No one attempts to address the wants, needs, and psychological desires of teachers.

Teachers do not feel they are part of an inclusive network. Nor do support staff people like secretaries, custodians, and cafeteria workers. Parents are another group left out of the loop.

All the more reason to begin a dialogue about team learning. School teams can create a learning condition that allows schoolpeople to lead a more sensory life. Teams provide newfound access to an opening into the flow of participatory creativity without attempting to overintellectualize the experience.

Schoolpeople should be granted the chance to celebrate the value of teams. Instead of being in a place where they are running away from the edicts of the school organization bureaucracy, they can run toward something that gives meaning to their work. Teams can afford the members of a school culture a common bond to uncover aspects of teaching and learning that need to be reinvented.

From a vision of the possible, the pieces of learning can be put together. Disjointed fragments of the school day like staff development, collaboration, and prep time can become topics of meaningful dialogue in school teams. Restoration of a vision can transpire when people are moved to share their dreams and aspirations about the ingredients required to create a quality school.

Dr. Deming realized that people have an intrinsic desire to learn, which is sometimes stifled by the organization for which they work. Just as children have different modalities of learning, adults learn in different ways and at different speeds. It is up to school leadership to design forums whereby individuals may achieve optimum learning. School principals, as well as other school leaders, cannot hope to address the rigorous issues confronting them without the assistance of the human resources that exist in and around the school campus. Leaders at school have no closed market on brain power. One of the themes in Douglas McGregor's *The Human Side of Enterprise* is that imagination, ingenuity, and creativity are widely distributed in the population.[2]

People want to engage in a search for meaning in their environment. They want to assume responsibility and find the nurturing, support, and collegiality of teams as a source of stimulation for further learning. The

---

LEARNING WINDOW 2.4
Leading Others, Managing Yourself

Effective Leadership

✔ Takes risks.
✔ Encourages innovation.
✔ Challenges people.
✔ Changes the basic metabolism of the organizational culture.

Adapted from Warren Bennis and Burt Nanus

cooperative spirit and "safe" conditions established within the ranks of teams allow people to explore possibilities of improving their own performance, growth, and productivity.

Teams will consistently outperform individuals. Team learning offers a full range for maximizing the available talent in the school environment. Teams traverse the known and unknown. Learning in teams can be obvious or subtle. Meaningful collaboration characterizes dynamic teams. It is the personal commitment made by team players that sparks them to recognize their need to contribute to the culture and to continue their professional development.

Teams are propelled by the anticipation of achievement. They offer individuals a real opportunity to make a difference. In addition, the best teams are fun to be part of: Everyone wants to make a contribution; everyone wants to stand for something. Everyone wants to lead a life of significant contention, solving problems and living and working with a positive outlook. Teams offer hope to those who feel otherwise disenfranchised.

LEADERS AS GUIDES ON THE JOURNEY

High-performance teams are an ensemble of players who are major characters in the movement toward a quality school. When people work in teams, they make a strong commitment to their fellow team members to play an active role in the process or product that is required. But they also make a personal vow to become a lifelong learner—charged, productive and self-sustained.

Schoolpeople of the contemporary world desire to become a versatile resource. When they are brought together in team dialogue, they promote creativity and generate energy. Meaningful dialogue is the tool for the most efficient use of the talents in a school. Leaders who promote such communication understand that past methods of manipulation of people have to give way to providing a forum for healthy exchanges about how to improve student learning.

School leaders can become important guides on the journey by building an audience fit to appreciate one another's contributions. The initial steps may include inviting those individuals most interested in creating change at the school site to participate in informal conversations on the topic. The school leader needs to be a skilled listener as well as a thoughtful contributor in these forums.

Through practice, team members will come to recognize the productive flow of creative dialogue. They will also come to discern how a collective vision of possible scenarios for school change is more powerful than a single vision for change. The message from the players must come from the heart as well as the head. And it can only transpire under an umbrella of trust.

The processes for improvement of schools rests with the active participation of teachers who possess a dual capacity for improving their personal learning as well as enhancing their professional seasoning. Schoolpeople bring a quiet power and authenticity to the table when they communicate about lifelong learning. They need to be included in the mix about improving teaching and learning at schools.

They also bring a relevance and urgency in their collective participation. Schools are about students. Learning is about students. Professional development is about students. Students are not a detour or interruption in the day; rather, they are the reason schoolpeople are at the site.

Leaders who focus on how to improve practices that help students are the ones who realize that teachers, paraprofessionals, support staff, students, and parents need to be included in communication about how to achieve quality in schools. Egos can be checked at the school steps, when dialogue opportunities begin that explore how to improve processes at the school. The leadership of the school that employs team dialogue acknowledges that powerful communication has nothing to do with status or hierarchy and everything to do with being a leader.

Many teachers, support staff members, parents, and even students crave the opportunity to have their voices heard. They have ideas and opinions about situations that occur in their daily activities. They also desire an opportunity to assume leadership roles on the campus. It is not fair for only principals and coadministrators to dialogue about change while leaving some of the most important players out of the interaction.

Schools improve when schoolpeople in the culture develop a common vision of the changes that needed. The journey toward the vision is fraught with ambitious, honest dialogue. Meaningful change happens when people get involved, influence others, and take ownership of the direction of the changes that are to be implemented.

While it is our American nature to place great faith in the achievements garnered by individuals in our history, the rewards of cooperative enterprise are even more spectacular because groups cannot be controlled. It is an uncertain experience, but one that helps connect the discrete, fragmented lives of schoolpeople.

Because it is an uncertain experience, many leaders may fear the process of rigorous dialogue. People who are in lines of authority that demand control in every aspect of the operation of a school will certainly fear the prospects of sustained, collaborative inquiry.

This brings up one of the paradoxes of school leadership. While many leaders in the school community profess to be forward-thinking, our schools continue to linger in a static zone. Schools are mired in rules and regulations that prohibit progressive revamping. Unfortunately, many leaders in the educational community hide behind these same rules to avoid implementing much needed changes in our schools. We have no one to point fingers at when we observe a weakening of social sympathy about education in our country.

The rich imagination of team communication knows no borders. People inscribe and take ownership for changes in the school with their words. School leaders who allow schoolpeople to define their roles in the new school paradigm recognize the importance of the personal growth aspect of speaking out. People create a new piece of the world for themselves when they are supported by visionary leadership.

If you want one year of prosperity,
Grow grain.
If you want ten years of prosperity,
Grow trees.
If you want one hundred years of prosperity,
Grow people.

—Ancient Chinese Proverb

QUALITY COMMUNICATION

Schools that embrace quality management principles and practices employ teams that deal with improving teaching and learning. The bottom line for quality schools rests with improving student achievement. Effective team communication gives meaning to the swarm of daily activities that take place at school in a given day.

The strength of a quality management school rests with the capacity of the individuals who make up the teams. When these individuals delve passionately into the team project at hand, they build lasting relationships that move the school farther along the learning curve. The real muscle of the school rests not with the internal organizational structure, but with the strength of the schoolpeople within the organization. Teams with poise, purpose, and passion create a true learning community because they believe in the work they do.

All paths are pretty much one in the same, but some are very special because they have heart.[3] In the best examples of team communication each person becomes both a teacher and learner. People learn to take ideas apart and put them back together—sometimes in a linear fashion and sometimes in a nonlinear process. It is a valued contribution to the process as long as the ideas spring from magical, lyrical places in the hearts and minds of the team players.

In quality management and non–quality management organizations, the area that people consistently enumerate as number one in impeding the building of trust and productivity is communication. The most forward-thinking organizations have only begun to explore ideas about how to improve communication and bring them to the surface.

It is apparent that face-to-face, open dialogue, where the sharing of insights and expertise by team members is recognized and valued, is a starting point for improving the general well being of the organization. The sharing of knowledge within the ranks of the organization is one of the most important activities that can happen.

Schools that are involved in the quality movement demand a constant push for continuous improvement and consistency of purpose. The guiding force that keep the schools on target is an uncompromising quest for quality at every corner of the campus. The best way to ensure that quality does permeate the system is not to talk about pressing concerns from a safe distance. If we really want schools to embrace restructuring, we must provide a forum for all schoolpeople to come together to deal with the pressing issues affecting student achievement. When those people gather from a variety of places to dialogue about creating quality learning, the entire school culture becomes more organic and, therefore, more human. Open learning in team dialogue is a perfect match for schools.

LEARNING WINDOW 2.5
Team Collaboration

✔ We care about team members and prove it by investing time and energy in listening to them.
✔ We are confident that together we can complete the task at hand.
✔ We are committed to helping one another. No one is alone on the team.

Adapted from Hendrie Weisinger

In reviewing Dr. Deming's concept of profound knowledge, when the human spirit is tapped, individuals understand their interconnectedness. As interconnected beings, they can learn to develop a shared consciousness that moves beyond the boundaries of past experiences or limitations and allows people to create a vision of the possible. Team dialogue offers each person an opportunity to open a special window to the soul.

Teams endear themselves with all the available talent in the system to produce the very best outcomes from their collaboration. The talent usually rests with the people who are most knowledgeable or have the most at stake in the project to be explored by the team. There is an efficacy of involving the individuals who have the most information or who are most directly going to be affected by the team project. First of all, it improves the quality of the product. And secondly, it leads to a wider audience acceptance, or "buy in," of the final plan.

THE PSYCHOLOGY OF COMMUNICATION

Everyone has ideas to impart on how to improve school life. Everyone wants to participate in the coevolution of a school. But how do we move from presenting information to giving meaning to the information? The following principles are important to remember about how humans process information:

1. Humans are social beings. It is through dynamic interaction with others that we establish rapport and begin to identify with a community.

2. Interaction with others tends to be value driven. Developmental relationships and a sense of who we are evolves when we communicate with our fellow human beings.

3. Cognitively we think through what we are listening to and speaking about when involved in discourse. We are constantly involved in a state of self-reflection.

4. Our preconceived notions influence what we are listening to and what we are communicating. These deeply ingrained assumptions color the world we see.

5. We process everything that is communicated at a conscious as well as an unconscious level. This means that we absorb information indirectly and also make meaning of information hours, weeks, and even months later.

6. Learning is developmental. There are predetermined paths of learning for everyone, beginning in our youth, yet each individual is at different stages at different times.[4]

Although the principles are presented as parts of the communication process, they tend to be processed holistically. We do not fully comprehend them if we linger too much on the pieces alone.

Active learning for schoolpeople is important for schools interested in pursuing quality processes. Teams won't be able to learn together by learning disparate ideas mechanically. Schoolpeople need to learn more than teaching strategies, or team building techniques, to successfully implement them. The best teams translate information into action, by practicing the application processes. All the while they are learning about themselves. New learning can be communicated externally as well as internally in this dynamic interplay.

WHAT IS TEAM LEARNING?

Team learning is all about new learning that takes place initially with an individual and ultimately in collaboration. It is reflective because it addresses what people are doing right now and asks them what they need to do to promote new learning. There is a specific team psychology that is present in team learning:

1. Relaxed people tend to be receptive to learning.
2. This leads to building on other people's knowledge bank.
3. Open listening is required to process new knowledge.
4. Members and the team engage in team dialogue to identify personal and team changes that need to be made.

THE ADVANTAGE OF REFLECTIVE THINKING

People tend to be more creative when they are relaxed. Rollo May wrote about how creativity tends to occur during pauses in life. He felt that to properly digest information and produce tangible results we must slow down and incubate it. Once the information is given personal meaning it can be transferred to others. But first we need to slow down and process the information. When we pause to reflect on our learning, we give it shape and substance.[5]

Everyone has done this with varying degrees of success in his or her lifetime. After immersing ourselves in an issue during the day and becoming frustrated because we were unable to formulate a logical solution, we wake in the middle of the night with an innovative solution. It has happened to all of us. All we needed was time to relax so we could be more receptive to learning.

Daniel Goleman, in his book *Emotional Intelligence*, calls this experience "flow." Goleman claims that people perform "at their peak while in flow." The hallmark of the relaxed zone of flow is that "emotions are not just contained and channeled, but positive, energized and aligned with the task at hand. The quality of attention in flow is relaxed yet highly focused . . . watching someone in flow gives the impression that the difficult is easy; peak performance appears natural and ordinary."[6]

Of all the massive changes wrought by the industrial era in our nation, none was more fundamental in transforming our world than the concept of time. The worldwide implication has been to produce more, faster, and with higher quality than before. As we enter the next millennium, we reflect and realize that we have been operating at breakneck speed for so long that we no longer recognize the value of slowing down.

Milan Kundera wrote a novel that is particularly relevant to this issue entitled *Slowness*. The novel is a tribute to the various aspects of slow, purposeful living. He celebrates the value of slowness and praises it in its various forms. One passage reveals how our fast-paced world has left us with a void for taking the time to appreciate one another. He suggests that we need to slow down to refocus our personal vision and take the time to connect with others to share our mutual visions. In another point in the story, Kundera signifies how, when we slow down, we have more clarity of thought. The example he presents to illustrate his point is that when we are walking at a rigorous pace, attempting to remember something, we automatically begin to slow down, shorten our stride, and, in many cases, come to a complete stop so that we can properly focus all of our attention and energy on the issue we are trying to sort out. When we slow down we unclutter and streamline our flow of thoughts. On the other hand, if we try to forget something, we speed up to escape ourselves.[7]

Slowness is to be honored. We need to extend ourselves to communicate in a rich support network that allows individuals access to savor the unspoiled beauty of ideas. We can enhance our dexterity with language. We can embrace the gift of our ear. People are the source of unexpected wisdom. Given time, they will deliver perspectives that can

```
┌─────────────────────────────────────────────┐
│              LEARNING WINDOW 2.6              │
│                   Slowness                    │
│                                               │
│   ✔ Listen attentively.                       │
│   ✔ Be open to divergent ideas.               │
│   ✔ Build on other people's knowledge.        │
│   ✔ Identify personal changes that need to be │
│     implemented.                              │
│   ✔ Reflect and slow down.                    │
│                                               │
└───∨────────∨──────────∨────────────∨──────────┘
```

broaden avenues, share a variety of options, and comment on the sounds of riveting change launched across a textured learning organization field.

When people are attracted to join together in collective merchandising of creative processes, they amplify the scope of their ideas. Teams are an eclectic merging of human power that unite from completely different directions to accept challenges and solve problems. The only clear characteristics of such team members are that they are extraordinary people with a strong creative vision. Sometimes they will initiate problem solving by taking a linear path. On other occasions they will proceed in nonlinear fashion after hatching ideas and tinkering with a series of concepts. The design they choose to achieve the end result is not important. The real currency of their endeavor rests with the final packaging of their partnership.

There is a special premium placed on timely, meaningful, slow interaction in the learning organization. Slowness adds value to the integrity of the team's intent. Slowness points out that good teamwork is noncompetitive. To achieve success in team ventures requires time for people to digest information, develop their capacity to fully comprehend variables, earn mutual trust, align their vision, and reason together.

Savoring the experience of ongoing learning gives teams reassurance to accept new challenges. Slowing down reinforces an integrity of intent. When we take the time to reflect on our understanding of elaborate issues, we fill gaps in our learning process. Reflection leads the heart. Sometimes we go too fast to promote learning, which is not a fast-track experience. An appreciation of slowness is an investment. It always returns dividends. One should not deny the self such a rewarding experience in the workplace. The simplicity of it all belies its vast power.

OPEN LISTENING

To listen effectively is to listen openly. How well are we prepared to listen to others without giving in to the urge to interrupt the speaker to interject own ideas?

Very often "people don't like to listen because it interferes with their talking."[8] To communicate effectively in teams there needs to be an assurance that people are really listening. I have employed the following two exercises in my school as source points for teams just after they have been organized to ensure that all team members are conscious of how important it is to practice open listening. It works with large or small groups and really hits to the core of the issue.

I ask each person to pair up with another individual sitting nearby. The person on the left is part of Team A and the person on the right is a member of Team B. I tell the entire group that Team A and Team B members are going to begin a conversation on the topic of "How to Improve Our School," but first I need to give specific directions to all Team A players. I then ask the Team A members to come forward and talk with me privately.

Once I am sure I am out of the listening range of Team B participants, I tell the Team A members that they are to employ a new behavior when they return to their seats next to Team B members. I then hold up a placard, out of the view of Team B players, which states:

IGNORE THEM

I tell the sequestered Team A people that, once a Team B person begins to talk, they think up ways of ignoring him or her. This may include looking at the ceiling, getting out a wallet and looking at old baby pictures, humming, or waving to friends across the room. I then return them expeditiously to their original seats and ask for the Team A and Team B members to begin their conversation on "How to Improve Our School."

Of course, there is absolutely no communication. Team B members become frustrated and bewildered. After several minutes, I stop them and ask Team B members how they feel. Many respond that they feel physically drained from the attitude of indifference. They also feel that no common ground exists because their message has not been received or internalized.

I then call Team B members forward and speak privately to them. The placard that I show Team B reads:

INTERRUPT THEM

Team B members are returned to their seats and I ask all Team A and Team B members to reinitiate their dialogue on the topic of "How to Improve Our School." Again, the premise of open listening disintegrates during the process.

When I stop the proceedings and ask Team A members how they feel, they typically respond that they are unable to organize their thoughts because of the constant interruptions, don't feel their ideas are valued, and stop attempting to communicate because they sense a lack of sensitivity on the part of their partner.

From this exercise, team members become sensitized about how important it is to listen actively to promote effective communication.

Open listening requires sensitive participation by all team members. How much a person is willing to contribute to the team dialogue depends on the message he or she receives from those in the audience. Therefore, it is the responsibility of each team member to create a free and open climate for people to express themselves. When people value and validate contributions, they open themselves up to more diverse points of view, new ideas that build on old ones, and broader approaches to problem solving.

BUILD ON OTHER PEOPLE'S KNOWLEDGE

Another technique I have used with teams at schools emphasizes the opportunity for an individual to organize and relate his or her thoughts on a topic without fear of being prematurely interrupted. This is the "mini-symposium."

The mini-symposium usually works most effectively in teams of less than twelve people. They sit in a circle, facing one another, and the facilitator asks for each of them to think about how they would respond on an educational topic related to the team enterprise they are involved in. For example, a team investigating how to improve report cards might be given the topic, "How would you incorporate rubrics on a new report card?"

After each person is given some time to reflect on how to approach the issue, the facilitator asks for a volunteer to share his or her insights. That person has up to four minutes to speak on the topic, *uninterrupted*. After finishing, the person to the immediate left has an opportunity to speak, and the process continues clockwise. Generally, I have the mini-symposium continue for two rounds, ensuring that each person gets at least two turns to speak.

When I stop the process, people generally want to go on. Although the mini-symposium may appear to limit interaction, it can actually serve to promote it. People learn to build on other's ideas because they have time to hear someone present his or her thoughts in detail and without interruption. When people are given time to slow down and incubate ideas, they gain deeper understanding and incorporate the new learning with their own insights.

We have social brains. We are always immersed in reflection on a subconscious level. When we have an opportunity to process our learning in a social context, such as that which exists in teams, we engage in a collaborative codependency of learning. When schoolpeople communicate effectively, the entire culture is elevated to a new, more people-valued level.

TEAM LEARNING AS AN EVOLVING DISCIPLINE

Team learning is an evolving discipline. This is not to say that communication in teams is a formal discipline, but that it is one more characteristic of the type Peter Senge refers to in his five disciplines.[9] Teams offer a unique opportunity to explore the contemporary landscapes of thought about how to improve schools. As invitational processes, they invite a liberation of thought for schoolpeople who can create innovative approaches to goals or other issues their team is charged with solving.

The rich texture of language flows through dialogue sessions. Words add dimensions, colors, subtleties, nuances, and vision to the mix. A cumulative wisdom arises when people dialogue about important issues. People are far and away more intelligent together than individually.

Effective communication serves to *link* people together. Much has been written about how our contemporary world has been relegated to "sound byte truths" and about an overall denigration of the spoken word. Some of this has to do with our impersonal, fast-paced world that has resulted in a society devoid of a personal touch. Previously diminished skills in effective use of language can be renewed in the context of team dialogue.

Apart from the literal context of the spoken word, there is an integrity in the men and women who have devoted their lives to the noble cause of teaching youngsters. Communication about important issues can move beyond the utilitarian possibilities of the original context and bubble with a creativity that stretches beyond the fences of the school.

Dr. Deming often spoke of the need to access the mind and heart of each worker. He felt that when people put their heart and soul into work, they achieve a rare level of self-discovery both professionally and personally. When people feel good about work, they feel good about themselves. People will put more into their efforts when they feel passionately about the contributions they are making and how those contributions are defining and shaping the culture of the organization.

Schools are experiencing a loss of credibility with society because we have failed to communicate effectively with our colleagues and our customers. The problems that dwell in the classrooms are capable of being solved only when we open doors to all schoolpeople so that they can speak with one another in meaningful forums about the true causes of our problems. Understanding one another leads to a greater understanding of the complexities of the concerns.

As schoolpeople begin to engage in team learning, they make a contribution to an evolving discipline. Elements of this discipline include a demonstration of faith in one's fellow colleague. People learn that, by working with and through each team member, an alliance develops. This alliance both bonds the people to each other and expands the vision of the school.

Another aspect of this discipline has to do with a creation of new energy. Schoolpeople become major players in an ongoing dance of energy and creativity. A powerful reflection is possible when people interact in professional dialogue in school teams. When they engage in inquiry, reflection, and analysis about school issues in a nonconfrontive forum, they gravitate toward a quality experience. A true community of learners emerges and grows when each person comprehends that he or she is an extension of the culture at large.

When teachers, principals, classified staff, superintendents, school board members, parents, and students speak and listen to one another, they reduce the monolith of bureaucratic lines of management into small, resolute pieces of human discovery. When we realize that we are all in the system together and that each person has something special to offer, an accepting, unifying voice emerges.

Still another piece of the discipline has to do with self-discovery. As individuals meet with fellow team members to consider issues, they discover variables within their own actions. They may reflect on their own specific endeavors, challenge personal beliefs and values, or take a hard look at how their goals fit with the team and school vision.

Self-discovery helps all individuals consider how their actions, intended or unintended, support team efforts to create desired outcomes. When people view themselves as agents of change, change is easier to accomplish. As people learn to speak authentically and honestly about how they can influence organizational change, they clarify their roles in the school culture. Reflection is a springboard for deeper, personal explorations of how people act in the context of daily school life. It gets to the source of how committed people are to change and how they will assist the culture in achieving concrete models of restructuring.

Changes in classrooms occur in schools that have a passion for learning. Everyone in the school has to have a determination that students will grow in their ability to read, write, compute, and solve problems. Schools have this focus when they are allowed to participate in powerful team dialogue and reflection about their practice. Yielding genuine improvement begins with the first conversation.

In review, aspects of the discipline of team learning include, but are not limited to

- Creating alliances with team members
- Discovering an energy source in team dialogue
- Linking, and making connections
- Employing active listening skills
- Uncovering possible resources that exist in others
- Personalizing the process of self-exploration
- Recognizing the interdependence of teams, and the school culture at large

Team dialogue creates a new, loose structure within the school framework that improves overall communication. Dialogue is an important tool by which to engage schoolpeople in articulation, examination, analysis, and reflection on pressing issues that affect the lives of those individuals who inhabit the school building. Dialogue fosters continuous learning by allowing participants to speak in open, honest, and authentic terms about methods for supporting one another and creating more effective and efficient learning communities.

UNCOMMON PEOPLE ON COMMON GROUND

High-performance teams don't do things differently; they do different things. Team communication brings schoolpeople together from diverse backgrounds and disciplines to work together to improve student achievement. They strive to raise expectations. They are a foundation on which the potential of every idea is built.

As communication improves in the educational community, schoolpeople better comprehend that the human imagination is our greatest untapped asset. Team members accept the role of becoming a lifelong learner by actively participating in the ebb and flow of team inquiry. Sharing craft knowledge and practicing active listening techniques open team members to an opportunity for compelling self analysis.

Team members feel comfortable when they know that information is open and accessible. They become enthusiastic learners in a receptive atmosphere. Schoolyard fences physically isolate schoolpeople from the real world outside. Sometimes they also serve to isolate people's ability to challenge old paradigms that exist *within* the fences. The very best teams are capable of looking beyond the confining walls of the schoolyard when they serve in team collaborations.

Collegiality and risk taking are by-products of creative teams. Profound team learning experiences occur when people are given a forum through which to question and examine routine practices adhered to in schools. Imaginative people bring an energy and life to teams. Margaret Wheatley, in *Leadership and the New Science*, reports that "because power is energy, it needs to flow through organizations. . . . We have seen the results of this flowing organizational energy in our experiences with participative management and self-managed teams. Those who are open to others and see others in their fullness create positive energy."[10]

When teams use every possible channel to produce quality goals, they consciously and unconsciously engage in behaviors that are consistent with creating a learning organization. If people want to challenge themselves for renewal, they can create conditions in their organization to promote a promise of transformational change.

Winning teams seek to challenge systems and structures within the school hierarchy that have not been confronted before. Teams are limited only by the capital of their collective imagination. Many of the rules that govern individuals in schools and school districts are not externally imposed; rather, they are imposed from within. We educators are quite adroit at self-inflicted paralysis. We are often the first to complain about

LEARNING WINDOW 2.7
Stem Questions to Improve
Communication at Your School

✔ How can we champion improved communication at
   our school?
✔ What strategies can be used to build on the learning
   of others?
✔ How can we incorporate "slowness" in our new learning?
✔ What communication schemes can we introduce to
   improve reflective practice?

a new idea when it is presented. How many times have you heard, "That won't work," or "We've already tried that before." In other instances, we provide only marginal effort and energy to inspire mastery in new projects and processes because "it is too much work."

The underlying benefit of creative people is that they have the ability to create interest in transforming schools with their imagination. Italian writer Anna Maria Ortese wrote these worlds about imaginations, which she chronicled as "magical realism":

> "There are moments in the life of the imagination—which, after all, is the life that all of us live—when everything you have ever thought before, even an instant before, is no longer of any importance, or at least stands perfectly still, and the only thing you see is reality. Yet the real, in that very instant, shows an unexpected dimension of itself becoming everything one might never have thought."[11]

There is a quality experience awaiting schoolpeople and students inside the walls of the schoolyard. Creative people have a knack of inspiring high levels of expectation when they interface with other creative people in high-performance work teams. However, individual imagination is not nearly enough to broker transformational change in our schools. One must also be able to communicate ideas and deeds in order to reach the corners of the entire school community. The words of change must be translated into action plans. Even then, constant communication must be nurtured among team members as the process moves through various stages of development and application.

Without the words—that is, engaging communication—meaningful change cannot be championed in our schools.

ENDNOTES

1. Robert M. Pirsig, *Zen and the Art of Motorcycle Maintenance: An Inquiry into Values* (New York: Morrow and Company, 1974).
2. Douglas McGregor, *The Human Side of Enterprise* (New York: McGraw-Hill, 1960).
3. Carlos Castaneda, *The Teachings of Don Juan: A Yaqui Way of Knowledge* (New York: Simon & Schuster (Pocket Books), 1968).
4. Renate Nummela Caine and Geoffrey Caine, "Understanding a Brain-Based Approach to Learning and Teaching," *Educational Leadership,* October 1990, vol. 48, no. 2.
5. Rollo May, *The Courage to Create* (New York: W.W. Norton and Company, 1975).
6. Daniel Goleman, *Emotional Intelligence* (New York: Bantam, 1995).
7. Milan Kundera, *Slowness,* Translated by Linda Asher (New York: HarperCollins, 1994).
8. Fred Pryor, *The Energetic Manager* (Englewood Cliffs, NJ: Prentice-Hall, 1987).
9. Peter Senge, *The Fifth Discipline: The Art and Practice of the Learning Organization* (New York: Doubleday, 1990).
10. Margaret Wheatley, *Leadership and the New Science: Learning About Organization from an Orderly Universe* (San Francisco: Berrett-Koehler Publishers, 1994).
11. Anna Maria Ortese, *The Music Behind the Wall: Selected Stories,* Volume I, Translated by Henry Martin (New York: McPherson and Company, 1995).

LEARNING WINDOWS

2.1 Scott Adams, *Dogbert's Top Secret Management Handbook* (New York: Harper Business, 1996).
2.4 Warren Bennis, and Burt Nanus, *Leaders: The Strategies for Taking Charge* (New York: Harper and Row Publishers, 1985).
2.5 Hendrie Weisinger, *The Critical Edge* (New York: Harper and Row, 1989).

CHAPTER

Building Blocks for Winning Teams

"If you have built castles in the air your work need not be lost; that is where they should be. Now put foundations under them."

—Henry David Thoreau, American author and naturalist

Winning teams do not just happen in any organization. They are the end result of effective communication from many corners of the school community. The successes of the team largely depend on the ability of leaders to communicate project goals and how they align with the schoolwide vision. The team members bring the project to life by interacting productively with one another to bring the aspirations of the team to fruition.

Unfortunately, many school principals have found it far easier to *direct* people than to *develop* them. As a consequence, many teachers, paraprofessionals, and parents go through the artificial routine of giving "bake sale" input to the principal on school matters and projects when the results are a foregone conclusion. They soon realize that they really have no true voice in the end results. Their involvement is superficial and they participate in a limited, nonrisking fashion. One would be hard pressed to call such an assemblage a team.

People in schools cannot be supervised, directed, or coerced into achieving excellence in team endeavors. Team learning offers the potential for personal stretching, self-reflection, and ongoing learning. When schoolpeople feel free to inquire and experiment on the job, they are fulfilling Dr. Deming's treatise on profound knowledge. They recapture the spirit of risk taking and learning that exits inside each individual, and they commit to learning lifestyle that balances work and personal growth. The intrinsic need for self-discovery creates an openness for personal transformation.

THE ADVANTAGE OF TEAMS

Winning teams can be a valued resource in the school environment. Everyone in the school culture is recognized as a potential creative source. One of the perpetual rewards of having high performance teams in schools is that they offer the possibility of continuous learning. If the leadership in the school values and validates team contributions, teams will continue to work together in developing breakthrough strategies that resolve high impact issues affecting school life.

Teams that take risks, learn from their errors, share important findings, and accept the reality of dealing with change are destined to become important learning resources. The more opportunities teams have to achieve short-term goals, the more they will gain self-confidence and accept even more arduous challenges. Success comes in small increments.

It is said that a successful team beats with one heart. Teamwork involves more "we" and less "me." While each person on the team is valued, it is the total blend of the individuals into one unit that makes the team important. While each person may have the opportunity to take center stage during some aspects of processes, it is the total amalgamation of talent on the team that ensures effectual results.

One of the very best illustrations of how this delicate balance between individual and team alliance is maintained is characterized in the grand old game of baseball. In baseball, the rules of the game declare that even the best player on the team rotates to take his turn at bat only once every nine times. In other sports like basketball, hockey, and football, clubs can go to the best player time and time again to score. In baseball, the TEAM is of paramount consequence. *Everyone* is expected to make a contribution. The community of the team is of utmost importance if they are to be able to win consistently over the long summer season.

Winning teams have two things in common: they employ an impressive ability to (1) listen and (2) communicate with one another. The successful completion of team projects depends on the proper coordination of tasks within the team ranks. Team players have to be able to analyze subassignments, develop strategies, acknowledge possible impediments, and plan for contingencies. Each of these likelihoods should be addressed sensitively and openly in order for the team to continue to remain on course and develop useful strategies for the projects they are charged with completing.

Abraham Maslow, arguably one of the two or three most important psychologists of the modern era, described how human beings communicate on five differing levels:

LEVEL ONE: The cliche or superficial level wherein individuals respond and acknowledge one another out of politeness.

LEVEL TWO: Involves two people speaking of a third party or object. Once again, there is no extension of sharing of the inner self in these conversations, which typically offer no substance or depth of insight.

LEVEL THREE: Once again, two people are engaged in a conversation, but this time the subject may be about more personal topics such as religion, politics, or family. At this level, one may reveal slightly more about oneself than in either of the previous two categories of human expression.

LEVEL FOUR: An increasingly deeper level of communication transpires here. Individuals may openly share their aspirations, sorrows, errors, hurts, and fears in this level, which uncovers who we really are.

LEVEL FIVE: On Maslow's fifth level an individual listens to others' deepest longings and disappointments and gives and receives love from others.[1]

In effective teams enterprises, people are often engaged in level four and level five experiences. Valuing fellow members and validating the hopes of those members is essential for the promotion of sustained, collective inquiry. A trusting environment is paramount for a team to venture into Maslow's latter levels of verbal engagement.

Winning teams employ attentive listening and reflective thinking practices at each meeting. They do not get "locked in a paradigm" presupposing that they hear what they expect others to say. Such a mind-set only produces fragmentation and miscommunication. When any team member makes a contribution, individuals demonstrate respect and offer credibility to the statement. All aspects of team dialogue—trust, respect, exploration, discovery, and insight—are in place and modeled.

High-performance teams recognize that there are two fundamental purposes for congregating and collaborating: The first is to increase self-knowledge, while the second is to increase organizational learning. When both occur, fascinating excursions into the highest levels of human thinking happen. Such an experience attests to the reality of Deming's high concept of "profound knowledge."

TEAMS ARE. . . .

Teams involve everyone working in the same direction. Every member pulls his or her own weight and lends support to those people who desire to be assisted. This feature of inviting help is an important notion. People on the team should be able to access help if and when they need it and be allowed to operate "interference free" when they don't. Not only are creative juices allowed to ferment in such a setting, but the trust level required for daily operation is reinforced.

Successes and failures are shared experiences in teams. As is the deep sharing of a passion to do an outstanding job on the project at hand.

Effectual teams test a wide array of learning strategies and techniques in order to resonate with confidence. They self learn the most efficient way of constructing a context for learning for their own team. Instead of an emphasis on individual cognition, social interaction is the spark that results in the creation of new learning. In team settings, the acquisition and application of knowledge is a concrete, social act. Teams define their learning in a social context. By employing skilled listening, observation, dialogue interaction, and self-reflection, teams determine their own problem-solving methodology.

LEARNING WINDOW 3.1
Good Team Practices

✔ Practice inclusion.
✔ Advocate win-win strategies.
✔ Live the calling of the school vision.
✔ Operate as risking, change agents.
✔ Model appropriate behaviors.
✔ Rely on the insights of colleagues to grow.
✔ Have trust and open communication.
✔ "By the hands of many, a great work is made light."

Information is always in a state of flux for team members because they are constantly accepting and processing new information from a variety of sources, which causes them to revise prior team knowledge. Hence, new knowledge causes a disequilibrium in the team environment, a prerequisite for change and growth in any organization. As new information is digested, it is placed in a context with other banked knowledge. Sometimes new knowledge is synthesized and other times it is allowed to stand alone.

TEAM PROBLEM-SOLVING PRACTICES

There are three major practices in the field of team problem solving. When used properly, they provide a rich environment for self- and organizational growth. These problem-solving practices are not some remote pedagogy that is inflicted by university professors in an ivory tower. They are common knowledge. We use them all the time in our everyday routines. It is only when we delve into the intricacies of each that they give the appearance of being highly complex.

The first, and most recognizable, practice is **Brainstorming.** This model was first developed and employed in the corporate world about seventy years ago and is acknowledged to be a very useful tool to generate a preponderance of ideas quickly. A primary rule of brainstorming is that all ideas tendered are accepted without making any sort of judgment on their usefulness, practicality, or quality.

The desired effect is to create a multitude of ideas within a limited window of time—anticipating that placing a plethora of ideas on the table, without taking the time to critique each one, will yield some new perspectives on the issue at hand. Brainstorming is from the school that "quantity can produce quality."

As a rule, brainstorming encourages high levels of participation, with an occasional flash of brilliant revelation. Brainstorming's main contribution in the vast majority of situations is to manifest a hybrid effect. Aspects of many ideas are found to be useful in generating a course of action that may lead to the eventual resolution of the problem or project. This concept fits perfectly with the philosophy of team participation. The adage that two heads are better than one translates to: While no single person has all the correct answers, everyone who takes part in the team enterprise has a piece of the answer to contribute.

Brainstorming powers ideas, but eventually they must be "filtered." The next two practices, **Analysis** and **Lateral Thinking,** are usually the

---

LEARNING WINDOW 3.2

"I would say that one cannot speak at all about linear progress. What we can speak about, however, is novelty and rules within randomness."

—*Ilya Prigogine (Nobel Prize Winner in Chemistry)*

---

next step in effective problem solving. Some academics may conjure intricate names for these practices, but they are very straightforward mediums of problem solving.

Analysis, or analytical thinking, places a heavy emphasis on logical and rational discourse. Unfortunately, so many school systems are locked into this mind-set that creativity is seldom allowed to surface in an analytical mode of team learning. Furthermore, school administrators, from site principals to superintendents, have typically received their formal university training in this mode. Consequently their approach to problem solving reinforces the way they were taught. It is hard to introduce the use of imagination and creative perspectives in schools when much of the educational community adheres to a safe "mainframe" approach. Old paradigms never seem to disappear from our education culture. How can we hope to become a learning community if we remain myopic about accepting new ideas?

My dismay about this state of affairs is clear to all visitors who come into my office. A large poster on the wall states my concern most eloquently:

"Schools are told not to do anything different and then graded on creativity."

Despite an obvious concern about creating a lockstep mentality, there is a time and place for analytical thinking in team enterprises at school. While analytical thinking is highly structured, there are times when it can be of value for teams. The most obvious is when teams need to focus on specific issues. In uniting their energy on one set of situations at a time, individuals can diagnose causes and then offer their individual hypotheses for a solution. This sequencing of processes places everyone on the same footing, receiving the same information at the same time.

Analytical thinking is a cool medium. Stages must be followed and uniformly processed, information must be collected and then dispassion-

---

LEARNING WINDOW 3.3

"Mediocrity paralyzes men's noblest impulses. After a certain level of the problem has been reached, legalistic, linear thinking induces paralysis, it prevents one from seeing the scale and the meaning of events."

—*Alexander Solzhenitsyn*

---

ately delivered to the next phase. Analytical thinking produces images of structured, deductive learning that may confine the innovative potential of individuals who compose the team.

Allowing time for idea development to incubate is assured in the analytical sequence of events. Inferences are made from the available data and then suggestions are presented for study. Eventually these suggestions are narrowed, by consensus, to a short list of good ideas or even a single idea, and the next step in the process is introduced.

When it works well, analytical thinking achieves closure when a possible solution is presented to the entire team and a final, mutually consented closure is created. Included in the process is the assessment of pertinent data, speculation on the validity of the data, debates about the practicality of the solution, and a group determination as to whether the results are really an improvement over the present condition.

Even then, the idea may need to be field tested, and the results of the field test may require the team to go "back to the drawing board" to devise alterations or even a new plan. This can be a most unfortunate experience. Teams spend a great deal of time and energy weighing a proper course of action, and the prospect of reconvening to revisit the process can be demoralizing. When teams feel that their efforts are locked in a sphere of inertia, they lose steam and credibility. The saying that "analysis leads to paralysis" fits the bill in such a dark scenario.

The rigorous process of analytical team reasoning offers no guarantees and is almost always extremely time consuming. Furthermore, innovation rarely finds the light of day if the processes in analytical thinking are strictly followed. However, the prospect of **Lateral Thinking** introduces a new dimension to team inquiry. Lateral thinking is distinct from analytical thinking because it asserts that there is more than one correct answer and more than a single way to accomplish a team goal successfully.

Lateral thinking is a hot medium. There is a depth and breadth to this process because it encourages the team to constantly refine, research, and redevelop ideas. In many ways it resists closure because it encourages ongoing social interaction. The forum is then available to other team members to join in producing the blueprint for the final scheme by elaborately plotting layers upon the original presentation.

Unlike analytical thinking processes, which have a defined grid to follow, lateral thinking flows with the dialogue of the team—leading to unexpected, innovative outcomes. Ideas are built upon other ideas as if the fire of knowledge burns in each team member. Team meetings become acts of daily faith for the team and their goals. A direct symbolism exists between the word *alchemy* and the hot medium of lateral thinking. Paracelsus, who lived in the sixteenth century, is widely acclaimed the first true alchemist. It was he who was quoted as having said, "Alchemy is the art which makes the impure into the pure through fire."[2] It is the burning force of high-minded team collaboration, which is often precise, intelligent, and magical, that provides the nourishing energy to propel a team on its mission to achieve its ultimate goals.

Winning teams will make use of all three processes—Brainstorming, Analysis, and Lateral Thinking—from time to time. It is vital to remember that effective teams are fused together by participating in the community of dialogue, which acknowledges collective learning as paramount to any process. Teams learn in many ways; their dialogue is the cord that binds them in harmonious learning and action.

Different players on the teams have various ways to approach problem solving. The wise facilitator will understand this and seek to find which of the three major problem-solving practices, or combination of them, fits the players' needs. The capacity of the team to communicate will be the essential tool to open the doors to future learning. Ambitious dialogue lends itself to free team members to frame and reflect upon appropriate strategies that will lead to new learning and innovation.

WHEN YOU HEAR HOOFBEATS
YOU USUALLY DON'T THINK OF ZEBRAS

When participants in teams are able to identify and release their full potential, both the effectiveness of the team and the entire school culture are advanced. The achievements of the team are proportionate to individual members' freedom to be creative within the ranks of the team. When schoolpeople are presented with an opportunity to work in a trusting culture, they have every opportunity to shape and develop their capacity for creativity.

Creative thinking, as the heading suggests, is all about looking at a problem outside the obvious line of thought. Every member of a team has the potential to be creative. Schools, like every other organization, need to "stop thinking in terms of 'creative' and 'noncreative' people, and see everybody as a potential creative source."[3] Creative people offer ideas as springboards for further study when teams are contemplating a course of action. This "springboarding" effect often expands the possibilities for solutions to team projects.

An unfortunate reality of contemporary schools is that problems are often solved just as they've always been solved. Team enterprises may be passed over by the school principal who is uninitiated regarding the potential of team learning, in favor of the expediency of an executive decision. It can be rationalized by the principal because it is less time-consuming and doesn't derail fixed lines of authority. However, such resolutions to school issues are not quality approaches. Teams are all about quality. If members of the school community are serious about incorporating quality management practices in schools, they must address the prospects of team learning in a forum that earnestly presents its attributes and possibilities.

Creativity in team processes can create an expanding world of high expectations for the entire school community. Creative thinking causes everyone to stop to examine routine school activities such as schedules of classes, grading practices, presentations of course work, and collegial partnerships. Creativity is unleashed in the hidden opportunities and unexplored possibilities that exist. New approaches to problems unearth new potential in schoolpeople.

Creative people should be viewed as a resource on the school staff. School teams can foster a shift in the mind set of linear and reductionist thinking that permeates the educational community. When one creative person moves farther along the learning curve, the entire team moves farther along the learning curve. When the team advances farther along the learning curve, so does the entire school culture. Schoolpeople are connected by a common language that swirls through the schoolhouse buildings. The spirit of learning abounds in the hearts and minds of people who are patiently awaiting the opportunity to be asked to make a contribution.

There is a force field of energy that creative people bring to teams. They assume leadership roles by generating quality initiatives to combat

---

LEARNING WINDOW 3.4

"New ideas need to be encouraged and stimulated. The aim is to invent new solutions. Apparently irrelevant material may lead the discussion into new and productive ground."

—*Vincent Nolan*

---

real problems facing the school. Multifunctional teams are composed of multitalented schoolpeople. They collect information, reach consensus, and plan actions by using a common vocabulary with uncommon talents. Each person on the team has the potential to be a creative force. Each person can add in increments to team gains in knowledge by contributing to the team alchemy and energy.

Winning teams are adroit at acquiring, creating, and transferring knowledge. In addition, they modify their actions and practice organizational learning behaviors, which leads to the development of fresh insights on issues and even the formulation of new knowledge that can be shared in the school. Creative organizations embrace change. They lay the foundation for a community of learners. Creative juices flow abundantly in these teams when they are aligned with the resonant vision of the school. When teams temporarily suspend assumptions about previous practices, they challenge one another to extend their boundaries and attempt to develop new and more innovative means of proficiency.[4]

GOAL SETTING

Successful teams set reachable goals. The desired result has to be realistically attainable, otherwise the team will lose energy and credibility. In addition, the human spirit, which can generate a wealth of powerful energy from within, is destroyed.

Reachable results are best accomplished when responsibility for completing subtasks is shared in the team. When a project is initiated, it is not enough to hope that a strong team commitment and focus will lead to exceptional results. It is of vital importance to constantly measure progress along the way to make certain that deadlines are met and the project remains fixed on course. Teams offer the promise of enlightenment, but they must be fine tuned continuously. Despite all their wonder, teams remain an uneasy paradise.

One strategy to employ in spurring the success of a team project is to conduct a "gap analysis." A gap analysis usually involves addressing the gap between the end goals of the project and the reality of where the team is currently. The team must use candor in reflecting on their current reality in order to decide where to go next. If the current situation requires new resources or a new path of thinking, this is the time to revise the strategic plan. This method of self-checking keeps the goals in sight and the process on the path to success. That is not to say that the course is necessarily going to be a smooth journey at all times.

Almost nothing goes according to plan. It is a fact that the first Apollo mission to the moon required constant gap analysis by the best brains in the aerospace community. It is a startling truth that Apollo was actually on course for about one percent of the total spaceflight. Thus, 99 percent of the time adjustments were being made to accomplish the goal of the lunar mission.[5]

Total commitment, organization of effort, and accountability are all important factors that must be melded to achieve the results that are truly desired. Effective communication between all players is critical to the success of a project. High levels of collaboration are mandatory, and the project must be internally integrated and aligned with the overall mission and vision of the school.

The process begins when the objectives of the project are presented at the school by one of the school leaders. This does not necessarily have to be the school principal. There are many leaders at a school. The wise principal will understand this and tap the abundant talent to achieve important results that will lead to improving the processes, which, in turn, will lead to transformational change in the school culture.

The true value to the project emerges when the team embraces the worthiness of the enterprise. It is essential that the team believe in the value of the eventual result and understand how it relates to the schoolwide vision. Furthermore, they must have confidence in the fact that they have the resources, information, and skills required to properly complete the project.

Setting the goals and instilling a sense of purpose for the team falls on the shoulders of the leadership at the school. A few of the questions the school leader needs to address include: Is this going to be a quality project? What do I need to add to the mix? How does my personal vision overlap with the long-range goal of the project? How do I motivate the players on the team to maximize their efforts?

Any ambiguity about the enterprise must be rooted out as much as possible. If there are multiple dimensions to the project, confusion is possible. Therefore, a healthy question and answer period is always recommended early on. The more clearly defined the goals, the better the eventual results. Team feedback helps define the goals as well as the work that will be required for quality results. The more team members choose to question and define the goals, the more the project is developed and shaped in their minds.

In fact, the diversity of the questioning will lend help on another front. As teams develop questions, they expend preconceived mental models and assume an "ownership" of the undertaking. "Buy in" is of paramount importance. When the goal of the project becomes a personal goal, success is on the horizon.

High-performance teams do not emerge from the dust. They emerge when people (1) have a clear vision of the goal; (2) buy in to the enterprise, and (3) collaborate effectively. Team learning is a difficult process. As stated earlier, Peter Senge recounts that, of the five learning organization disciplines he chronicles in his book *The Fifth Discipline*, team learning is the most arduous to master.[6] This is because there are so many interwoven personalities, possibilities, and paths of process that there is no "clean methodology" to employ and no road map that ensures success.

This "messiness" exists in even the most successful teams. Only the most venturous and visionary leader, as is skillfully depicted in the following excerpt, will attempt to make full use of the possibilities of a team enterprise.

> . . . It seemed to her (Ayla, a newcomer to the tribe) that it was more difficult to lead a group of people who believed everyone . . . had the right to speak out and be listened to. . . . It could become very loud and noisy when everyone had an opinion and did not hesitate to make it known, but Talut (the leader) never allowed it to go beyond certain bounds. Though he was certainly strong enough to have forced his will on people, he chose to lead by consensus and accommodation instead. He had certain sanctions and beliefs to call upon, and techniques of his own to get attention, but it took a different kind of strength to persuade rather than coerce. Talut gained respect by giving respect."[7]

—Jean M. Auel, The Mammoth Hunters

INDIVIDUALS AS PART OF THE TEAM

To achieve extraordinary results, as a team, a constant focus on the final outcomes is required. In many instances, school teams tend to lose sight of their purpose when they allow the process to become an end unto itself. Synergistic collaboration in a team is meaningful when deadlines are fulfilled and members think they have made important contributions. The best method to encourage future team endeavors is to build upon the successes of past team efforts.

The following learning organization worksheet is a starting point for individual reflection about how to best work in teams. It is also a check sheet for school leaders who wish to fulfill their roles as a steward.

LEARNING ORGANIZATION WORKSHEET

I work best in an environment that includes (e.g., behaviors of others, timing, communication, accountability, authority):

- ◆
- ◆
- ◆
- ◆

My team members require these things in a supportive environment:

- ◆
- ◆
- ◆
- ◆

Place an * beside the 2–3 items that you wish to specifically address.

Learning organizations are risk systems that promote a greater sense of collaboration. People with different work styles and strengths (for example, harmonious, self-directing, achievement oriented, creative, analytical) can work together so long as they share the same vision and goals. Their diversity is a strength that drives the undertaking. Different approaches to a problem can yield powerful insights and uncommon results.

Team learning promotes a deep sense of civic responsibility. Members of teams feel that their efforts can elevate the everyday lives of all the people who populate the campus. For school leaders, few acts have more enduring impact than building a foundation of core values and creating a framework of unlimited trust. Trust and creativity are powerful partners.

A learning organization requires school leaders to be willing, on a continuous basis, to share their own vision, model a commitment to the vision, and welcome divergent points of view. When people feel free to participate in the conversation about how to improve their school, they become an omnipotent resource. In such a free environment, all things become possible. Effective teams are motivated to accomplish goals when they feel trusted and appreciated for their contributions. The most important resource in any organization is the human resource. The opportunity for achieving accelerated "learning is greater today than ever before. In an increasingly dynamic, interdependent and unpredictable world, it is simply no longer possible" for any school leader to pretend to have all the correct answers.[8]

FROM PARTS TO WHOLE

Basic principles of interdependence exist for all living systems in the natural world—the desert or the sea, for example. The same can be said of human organizations. After all, human beings are nothing more than large organisms.

The word *organization* comes from the Greek word "organon," which depicts the premise of a group of organs functioning together, as an entity. Hence, when people commit to work together they fulfill a holistic, organic enterprise. Recently the school intelligentsia have joined with the rest of the world in the development of an appreciation for the concept of "systems thinking," or an appreciation of the whole.

Research findings report that lives of teachers and principals are "characterized by brevity, fragmentation and variety. During an average day, for instance, a teacher or principal engages in several hundred interactions."[9] It is only when we view these interactions in a holistic context that we gain real meaning from them and see how they align with the overall vision of the school. On a broader scale, we live in a world of many wide continents and large oceans—varied languages, cultures, and political beliefs. However, when viewed from a distance in space, we appear to be one single society, one community of human beings. Schools can also be viewed from a certain distance as a single society—a learning community.

A rudimentary fact of life is that organisms are part of a large, interdependent web. We, in schools, bring this interdependence to life on a daily basis. Schoolpeople—the students, teachers, parents, support staff, and administration—work together to complete an organic, interdependent school culture. When we view the interactions of the players as a whole, we gain important insights and perceptions about the value of the blend.

Without a clear sense of vision or purpose, we can lose our way in the maze of multiple interactions in the school day. Our collegial ties keep the organizational ship afloat and our humanity helps us to reenergize and renew. The prevailing vision of school teams keeps the culture together and on course.

Teams are a microcosm of the organization. Networking in teams maximizes the overall effectiveness of the school. Teams are engineered to remove isolation, which impedes productivity. Teams offer a support system so that staff members do not have to battle obstacles single-handedly. Furthermore, teams offer an enabling structure, so that knowledge can be effectively shared.

Teams are inclusive. They are designed to involve the entire school community. The constituencies of teachers, parents, students, support staff, and administration are all instrumental for productive change processes to occur. When teams function in a networked fashion, they develop and shape a shared language for holistic action.

FROM HIERARCHY TO NETWORK

A striking property of teams is their relationship with the total school culture. Dynamic, self-directed teams are not part of the old hierarchial order. This is because effective school teams are part of a transformational change model.

Teams offer a powerful advocacy for reform by generating a "respected voice." When team empowerment is given lip service by leaders, or teams see their projects "massaged" by the school principal to meet his or her needs, the vision of the school deteriorates. When teams are not empowered, the vision of the school is eroded. It can slip away, day by day, and with it the meaning that connects all the individuals to it.

Leaders of quality organizations share information and knowledge with teams to expand their level of responsibilities. They understand that a school has a broad distribution of talented people, as in any other organization. Therefore they advance the training of staff members, coaching them to exert their talents and insights.

LEARNING WINDOW 3.5
Contemporary Leader's Cascade of Attributes
to Promote Effective Teams

✔ Share information and knowledge.
✔ Coach to develop new leaders.
✔ Become stewards of a trusting, open environment.
✔ Support without supplanting authority.
✔ Model (walk the talk).
✔ Assume the role of teacher and learner.
✔ Frame tasks.
✔ Operate as change agents.
✔ Become excellent listeners.

Top-down principal archetypes still remain, but, hopefully, they are a dying breed. A new wave of school principals, trained in valuing people, is rapidly becoming the majority, and these individuals have assumed the role of movers and shakers in schools. Instead of allowing the old school paradigm to define them, they have embarked on a journey to define the new school paradigm. It is the fervent hope of this author that these individuals are introduced to quality management principles and practices either through university credentialization training or by professional staff development.

Fresh perspectives on school leadership are required to assist educational reform in our country. Quality schools are needed and new leaders are required who will be able to close the gulf that separates the vision of the school and the current reality of the people who work in schools.

Comprehensive change is a team effort. Teams create and nurture an unbroken thread of meaning for school culture. When talented people are encouraged to find solutions to perplexing issues, new territory is opened. Teams expand the craftsmanship, integrity, and intelligence of the entire organizational culture.

When individuals gather in a team campaign, the members have to believe in the importance of their team's contribution to the wider organization. Dynamic team undertakings are quality-inspired. Members of such teams recognize the unalloyed benefits of collaboration. The quality of the end result of the final product is greater than the sum of the parts. Drawing upon the intrinsic desires of each member to do a better job for the common good outweighs all other rewards. The "mosaic of moments" of introspection, passion, and learning that occurs in valued teamwork experiences causes an uplifting and contagious shift in the focus of the school.

The shift from a passive, compliance-led culture with paralyzed leadership, to one that embraces networking and customers, can transpire only when schoolpeople internalize commitment to the vision and identify with the values and mission of the school. When people journey along the learning curve to emerge as passionate players and energized thinkers, the school metamorphosizes into a living and breathing learning organization.[10]

BUILDING BLOCKS

The shift from hierarchy to networks is best modeled in team dynamics. In high performance teams, value is associated with embracing processes and sharing information in an open fashion. But how do teams arrive at this destination? It is a reality that there are some individuals in each school who are not motivated to change. Others are intent at sabotaging any efforts to reinvent schools. How does one get these individuals to participate and collaborate in a positive matter?

Some rudimentary building blocks for team learning are described below.

Strategies

In clearly defining the limits of the team at the outset, a tone of impartiality is introduced. When the team agree to establish a policy of how they will operate, many potential conflicts are reduced and everyone is placed on an equal basis to participate. Some examples of sound ground rules are

- Elect a facilitator, recorder, and timekeeper.
- Establish time limits on debates.
- Agree upon how to "critique" ideas without making disparaging remarks about individuals.
- Establish deadlines.
- Elect subchairpersons for extremely complex projects.
- Encourage different points of view.

- ♦ Ask open-ended questions.
- ♦ Use brainstorming techniques.
- ♦ Clarify and rephrase comments.
- ♦ Reserve your own views.

Facilitation

The facilitation of team meetings is of extreme importance to the cause of effective team performance. The following guidelines are presented to clarify the promise of effective facilitation:

Basic Principles
- ♦ Focus on the situation or issue, not on the individual.
- ♦ Encourage participation from everyone.
- ♦ take the initiative to improve processes by making suggestions to increase productivity.
- ♦ Lead by example.

Preparation
- ♦ Set convenient time and place for the initial meeting.
- ♦ Preplan future meetings.
- ♦ Invite team players.
- ♦ Establish an agenda.
- ♦ Establish ground rules.
- ♦ Define the purpose and goal(s).
- ♦ Ask for feedback.
- ♦ Provide needed information.

Disruptive Behavior
- ♦ Remain calm.
- ♦ Commend those participating with acceptable behavior.
- ♦ Reference ground rules.
- ♦ Attempt to refocus team.
- ♦ Acknowledge passion displayed by individual.
- ♦ Take a break from the proceedings.

Targeted Facilitation
- ♦ Follow the agenda.
- ♦ Allow the team to work through debate as much as possible.

LEARNING WINDOW 3.6
Stem Questions to See If Your Team Is on
Track to Becoming a Winning Team

✔ What good team problem-solving practices are we
following?
✔ How are we modeling inclusion of diverse ideas?
✔ How do we network effectively?
✔ What recent team project have we completed that I
am most proud of?

♦ Ask questions about the focus when the team strays.

♦ Reinforce constructive contributions and behaviors.

♦ When conclusions are reached, move on to new territory.

♦ Summarize progress periodically.

♦ Address follow-up issues by listing "action items" and identifying
individuals on the team who are responsible for completing them.

♦ Evaluate the meeting.

♦ Thank the team members for participating.

♦ Establish the date for the next meeting.

Teams do not become winning teams overnight. A good facilitator
can nurture a team by reinforcing behaviors just received and commit to
a position of "noninterference" unless absolutely necessary. Being a good
facilitator means not pushing the team to extremes while allowing them
to self-seek a collective balance. An energy flows through each team. It is
the wise facilitator who understands the importance of remaining outside
the dynamics of this energy force as much as possible. The building blocks
for effective teams come with patience and a lasting faith in people.

Teams achieve success by sharing power within the ranks of the membership. They draw strength from one another as well as from their inner
awareness. Team members gain energy from personal accomplishments
and the accomplishments of the entire team enterprise. The immense
power of the psychology of teams is unleashed when each member realizes
the interdependent connections of all team relationships. Effective school
teams are able to come to grips with their reality, make meaningful contributions to the school culture, and understand how the patterns of their
goals intersect with the vision and goals of the entire learning community.

ENDNOTES

1. Abraham Maslow, *Toward a Psychology of Being* (Princeton, NJ: D. Van Nostrand, 1962).
2. Kathleen Cambor, *The Book of Mercy* (New York: Farrar, Straus and Giroux, 1996).
3. Vincent Nolan, *The Innovator's Handbook: The Skills of Innovative Management* (New York: Penguin, 1989).
4. David A. Garvin, "Building a Learning Organization," *Harvard Business Review*, July/August 1993.
5. James Belasco, *Teaching the Elephant to Dance: The Manager's Guide to Empowering Change* (New York: Penguin, 1991).
6. Peter Senge, *The Fifth Discipline: The Art and Practice of the Learning Organization* (New York: Doubleday, 1990).
7. Jean M. Auel, *The Mammoth Hunters* (New York: Bantam, 1991).
8. Peter Senge, "The Leader's New Work: Building a Learning Organization," *M.I.T. Sloan Management Review*, Fall Issue, 1990.
9. Roland Barth, "A Personal Vision of a Good School," *Phi Delta Kappan*, March 1990.
10. James E. Abbott, *Managing at the Speed of Light: The ABCs of TQM for Schools* (Boston: American Press, 1998).

LEARNING WINDOWS

3.2 Ilya Prigogine, "As a Scientist," *New Perspectives Quarterly*, Spring 1992.
3.3 Alexander Solzhenitsyn, *A World Split Apart* (New York: Harper and Row, 1978).
3.4 Vincent Nolan, *The Innovator's Handbook: The Skills of Innovative Management* (New York: Penguin, 1989).

CHAPTER

Team Leaders

Advice to Leaders:
"Don't act like someone who's got all the answers. God is the only one with all the answers, and He's not telling.

—Anonymous

Quality organizations require people with special leadership skills and talents. Accountability for successful outcomes of projects falls directly on the team leader's shoulders. Therefore, additional responsibility rests with the leader to make certain that processes flow smoothly, deadlines are achieved, and a meaningful conversation forum has been structured to ensure that all members of the team have had ample opportunity to express their ideas regarding the completion of the project.

If the team fails in any of the above-mentioned areas, a trail of blame may well lead back to the designated person in charge of the project. Should a team fail to produce expected results, an implied element of poor leadership may even surface. The concern may be that the leader was not able to properly motivate or effectively tap the existing talent pool.

Therefore, the team leader has a vital role to play as motivator, manager, mentor, and maximizer of team potential to accomplish distinguished results. As has been previously mentioned, team dialogue is a messy proposition. However, the more often team members engage in responsible dialogue, the better they function.

Dialogue is the enabling tool that supports teams as they strive to explore necessary developmental strategies which, in turn, lead to uncommon breakthroughs. As people simultaneously learn from one another and

---

LEARNING WINDOW 4.1
Leading Change

✔ Change is driven by individuals
✔ High levels of collaboration are required
✔ Decision making is shared
✔ Change in schools is predicated in the belief that all students can achieve
✔ Opportunities for dialogue and reflection are provided by leaders in the school

---

plan with each other, they unleash potential resources that may have fallen dormant within the psyche.

Team leaders capture "group eagerness" and translate the confident excitement that is generated by participation into meaningful processes. Team leadership involves coaching, inspiring, rewarding, and leading people. In addition, team leaders have the added charge of launching the process and guiding it through various stages until it is completed. Add to that the reality that each team member is a participant in the task that the team is expected to complete. Therefore, leaders have the dual task of soliciting full participation by everyone while contributing their own thoughts and suggestions about how to improve the final team product. They face the dilemma of walking a fine line between advocacy of their own ideas while being receptive to the opinions of others.

Team leaders must be able to see the whole picture. They establish the framework that allows the team freedom to modify and refine the project and support team decisions. Leaders of teams are well organized and possess high levels of energy. However, the most important attribute of team leaders may well be that they are excellent listeners.

Skillful listening is an important ingredient in the mix of talent required for successful team leadership. Those individuals who are able to maintain a healthy equilibrium between advocacy, inquiry, and attentive listening are both gifted and valuable. It is important that leaders, in their attempt to maintain this balance, remember they are responsible for the way in which the team players work together as well as the ultimate results of the team effort.

ACTION PLANNING

Understanding "team psychology" is imperative for team leaders to achieve success with their project. The ability to set aside one's own agenda for the good of the team is essential. The primary purpose of the team collaborative is to bring the fruits of their labor to a successful conclusion. The secondary purpose of any team effort is to explore new information that may be useful to other emerging projects or simply to share with everyone in order to develop a deeper learning within the entire organization.

The following excerpt from the Tao Te Ching offers special insights on higher performance team leadership.

♦ Team members who influence others are considered coaches.

♦ Team members who know themselves are considered intelligent.

♦ Those who facilitate the work of others have strength.

♦ Those who, themselves, lead have character.[1]

Instead of concentrating their efforts on differentiation within the team, leaders are always evolving, attempting to become self investigative and principle centered. They tap into the swirl of energy created within the team to surpass themselves, move beyond previous performance limitations, and clarify their quest for lifelong learning.

Team leaders who commit to self-managed roles are models for actualized team behavior. Team leaders ask for contributions by others to address concerns. In an ideal situation, teams talk over what they need to work on and with whom they need to engage in order to complete the task. From such interaction, specific team goals are devised.

Goals are the beginning point for an action plan focus as well as the team's desired end result. Unless the goal is of an extremely complex nature, it should be defined at the initial team meeting. At that meeting, each team member should have an opportunity to ask clarifying questions and be given ample opportunity to dialogue with fellow members about the goals and how to attain quality results.

The dialogue session is important for two substantial reasons: Team members can (1) gain better insights about how the goal of the project applies to them and the school culture and, (2) "buy in" to the overall project. Team leaders understand the second point very well. If people commit to a goal, it is no longer "your goal"; it belongs to the entire team. The more the team feels an ownership to the process, the more optimized the level of team effort.

LEARNING WINDOW 4.2
When Devising an Action Plan

✔ State expectations
✔ Establish a method to measure achievement of the goals.
✔ Present time lines and a definitive deadline
✔ Suggest periodic self assessments (gap analysis)
✔ Identify additional resources required to properly complete the project
✔ Establish responsibility among participants for sub-projects

---

Winning teams evolve from a mutual, ongoing learning experience. There is no line of demarcation between those with rank in the organization and those without rank. Working together under an umbrella of trust, with a shared vision of the goal to be achieved, is vital. The open communication element suggested at the initial meeting is important to set the tone for future proceedings. As people dialogue about milestones and measurable goals, their fears about processes are alleviated.

Action planning reduces preconceived fears. Team members come to realize that the end product of the enterprise is not all up to them. The knowledge that the project is divided among others serves as a source of liberation. When all team members promise to work to the very best of their ability on their portion of the project, it energizes the entire team to make the same commitment to the whole cause. No one wants to let colleague down.

An intellectual intensity and integrity develops as team members acquire a dexterity with dialoguing. They learn to recognize special abilities and talents in others while stretching and surpassing themselves. Even in groups with dissimilar backgrounds, communication cuts across old boundaries and frees people to view teammates with newfound respect.

TEAM MOTIVATION

What is a good team? How do you build it? How do you know if it is good? What kind of leaders help make teams successful? These are questions that have subjective answers. For the most part, effective teams are composed of people who are emersed in self-directed learning. And good team leaders are role models for lifelong learning.

The opportunity for personal growth has a direct link to team successes. Team members are always looking for opportunities to support the learning of others and increase their own sphere of knowledge. Team leaders are always actively involved with asking the question, "What kind of leader do I want to be?"

Team members pump each other up. They are stimulated by inquiry and reflection. They are supportive and trusting. And they are motivated by the prospect of embarking on projects. But how do teams grow to become a center of energy and excitement?

Leadership at the school and leadership within the team ensures that some special conditions exist so that they can bond into a collective and forceful powerhouse. It is the person closest to the team activities who must assume the role of steward for the support of conditions to maximize overall effectiveness. That responsibility falls directly on the shoulders of the team leader. The team leader buoys the team experience by making certain that it operates with openness and flexibility. Furthermore, the leader ensures that the team has independence to pursue issues and autonomy to make important decisions regarding project outcomes.

The leader also keeps the team aware of emerging conditions that may affect deliberations and consistently provides the team with access to pertinent information they require. Finally, the leader always acknowledges the importance of the people who serve on teams.

The proper motivation of team members is an interesting and sometimes elusive conversation. In reality, the greatest source of motivation for any individual in any type of organization stems from personal satisfaction. People tend to be motivated by their intrinsic desire to do a good job. Dr. Deming held this to be one of the most important tenets of a quality organization.

The notion that recognition of accomplishments by teams and team members in schools is important. Some ideas for recognizing the efforts of team players that I have used include

- Write individual personal notes, expressing your appreciation for a job well done.

- Have a special recess or lunch period inviting school personnel and parents who have served on a team to recognize their accomplishments.

- Offer verbal compliments, always a plus.

- Find creative ways to "free up" all team members for an afternoon on school district time.

- Take recess duty for them.

The principal of the school may set a tone for team achievements. However, it is the team leader who gets involved in the nuts and bolts aspects of team interactions. Team leaders let the members know that what they are doing is important and appreciated. When team leaders are enthusiastic about a given project, provide adequate time and resources, and acknowledge achievements, people are willing to take on even the most challenging projects.

Schoolpeople have their personal desires, but also their needs. Team leaders can address these needs to reap the greatest dividends from the available talent pool. The school organization must always place people first; people have to know that they are valued. When people feel appreciated, they will exceed all prior expectations.

Team learning is a collaborative enterprise. Each player on the team should be recognized for his or her contributions. The cornerstone of self-directed teams is comprised of the total effort of individuals who are role models for self-directed learning. When teams are motivated, they grow. Individuals in team collaborations generate good ideas, support one another, and strive to improve interpersonal relationships. Innovations grow and multiply as people in the school tap into the entire learning culture. Team leaders recognize that the patient nurturing of individuals in the school culture is crucial for successful team enterprises. When people feel validated, they become "keepers of the torch" for ongoing learning and exceeding expectations. This is the stuff that learning organizations are made of.

FACILITATING THE MEETING

A team leader should be interested in bringing people together to take decisive action on a project. The leader should be adroit at facilitating meetings, attending to details, and invoking avenues of communication inside as well as outside the school channels. Leaders have an ability to see the larger vision of the school, are excellent listeners, desire to help others complete tasks, and are comfortable with taking the initiative. In addition, they serve as the contact person, maintain team correspondence and records, and are not given to easy detraction by popular opinion.

The issue of popularity is an important one. Being a team leader is not a popularity contest. Those individuals easily swayed by others should never consider accepting the demanding role of team leader. What would have happened if Moses had stopped and taken a poll while traveling across Egypt? How far would he have gone? Would his vision have come to fruition?

Team leaders clarify roles, draft improvement plans, access and present important data, establish an agenda, receive feedback from team members, and keep the theme of the project foremost in the minds of the team members. The full range of possibilities for each team is strung together by a series of interactions that are established at the initial team meeting.

THE FIRST MEETING

The following sequence of activities incorporates elements that will ensure high levels of productive interaction and help define a quality final product for the project.

- ♦ **Pre-planning:** Arrive early and pretest any audiovisual equipment you may wish to use as part of the meeting. Write out the agenda on a flip chart. Always print rather than use cursive writing. Make sure the seating arrangements are conducive to face-to-face interactions. Make a final check on other handouts, refreshments, or backup items that will be required.

- ♦ **Greet participants:** Welcome members personally as they enter the meeting room.

- ♦ **Beginning:** Establish the importance of timeliness. Time is one of the most important resources at a school. Ask for people to be prompt to meetings so they do not interfere with the schedules of others. Begin on time and end on time.

- ♦ **Ice breaker:** An ice-breaker exercise is always valuable to get people to talk with one another. The more fun people have in these activities, the more they will be likely to feel relaxed and open. The more relaxed they feel, the more likely they will be to make a contribution.

- ♦ **Self-introductions:** It is always a good idea to have individuals introduce themselves to the team. They may also be asked to tell how their vision of the school can be enhanced by the successful completion of the team project.

- ♦ **Team purpose:** The team leader should review the purpose of the team project and how it is aligned with the mission of the school.

- ♦ **Define roles:** Once the purpose of the team has been established, it is good to open up the proceedings to dialogue. People may wish to talk about how they see their contributions being made, to determine which other resources may be important to employ, and to make inquiries of the team leader with regard to specific concerns they may have about the project.

♦ **Ground rules:** Have team members create ground rules they feel are necessary to allow the team to function on an optimum level socially. This may include items such as one person speaking at a time, raising hands to be recognized to speak, and roles within the team such as secretary or facilitator.

♦ **Evaluations:** A final aspect to be reviewed is how to best determine effective evaluations of team meetings.[2]

♦ **Conducting the meeting:** The leader should make eye contact with everyone. Speak with conviction and show enthusiasm for the project. The team leader is a team member but is also a role model. The leader's job is to help the team work its way through processes to be sure there is ample opportunity for participation and inquiry, inviting contributions from everyone.

♦ **Follow-up:** The team leader should be accessible to everyone and address any follow-up items that are unresolved.

DECISION MAKING

How are the very best decisions made? Modern team decision making has moved away from voting and into the realm of consensus making. Quality decisions require a new approach that is inclusive and participatory. The participatory aspect of reaching consensus is grounded in the fact that when everyone's ideas are incorporated in reaching a final decision, the axiom that all of us are smarter than any one of us is most evident. The real strength of achieving team consensus lies in the open communication that develops. By recognizing and validating the importance of collegial contributions, inviting diverse perspectives, and opening visions of possible courses of action, all team members examine self-assumptions and move beyond any single perception of the issues.

Consensus lends to reflection. When team members listen to others, solutions are reached by a mutual integrity. People are happy to accept a solution when they know that their point of view has been considered, reviewed by colleagues, and may be a piece of the final results. In consensus building, it is assumed that everyone has a piece of the solution, while no one has *all* the answers.

Consensus is achieved when everyone can say: "I believe I understand your point of view." The final resolution is deemed to be one that is best for the entire school culture. People can "buy in" to the final consensus of the team and support it because it has been achieved in a collaborative process in an open forum.

Consensus, built into the school culture, is a nonthreatening, creative approach to problem solving. Team players value the engagement as well as the opportunities for reflection and inquiry as learning experiences. Consensus also serves as an important "linking" device. When people reach common outcomes on issues, they recognize how they influence others and see the value of interdependence in applications outside the team, such as team teaching, student groups, serving together on school advisory boards, and seizing future opportunities to collaborate on inventive teaching practices.

OPEN SYSTEMS

Teams, like quality management systems, are open. They are always looking to make connections with how they can align themselves and their project's with the overall vision and mission of the school. Teams also may peripherally address many internal issues in the school. They can influence improved practice among teachers, generate ideas for increasing parent participation, strive to continuously examine best educational practices, or function as a support system for collegial interaction, risk taking, and professional development.

There is much lip service given in educational circles to school reform efforts. Team leaders understand how effective teams can address true transformational change. Team leaders have a responsibility to create conditions within their own team's that encourage them to be as productive as possible. Lee G. Bolman, in *Leading with Soul*, states: "When people feel a sense of efficacy and an ability to influence their world, they seek to be productive. They direct their energy and intelligence toward making a contribution. . . ."[3]

People evolve as individuals as well as team members as they move through four stages of development:

+ What do I want?
+ How can I make a meaningful contribution?
+ What have I gained from this experience?
+ What possibilities exist for my future participation?[4]

The most insightful team leaders realize that successful teams are ideal work systems because they present the opportunity for personal as well as professional development. W. Edwards Deming could not have crafted it better: When people recognize their own potential, they tend to be more open in their behavior toward everyone. For schools to take up the notion of employing quality management practices, one point of embarkment may well be in growing team leaders who will be well versed in the practices of team learning.

MICRO MANAGEMENT

Once a team enterprise is initiated, leaders cannot micromanage the team or interfere with mutually agreed upon team processes. If teams have been granted an opportunity to take the lead in resolving an issue, both team leaders and school level administrators should avoid meddling with the outcome. This is important to remember, especially if the team is going through a turbulent period.

Leaders on the team are both team members and stewards of agreed upon processes. They should offer insights and assistance for the team only if asked. Any interference would only lead to distrust and the eventual demise of any effective team efforts at school. The power of teams is derived from the experience of collaboration in a trusting environment.

Team leadership cultivates a framework for people to begin to think about things differently than they have in the past. Leaders promote a level playing field for equal access to information through dialogue. Thought processes are expanded because leaders assume that people have valuable information to share. They know that the human imagination has no boundaries. Dialogue episodes in teams are part of a continuous learning cycle. Learning, in teams, is part of continuous, critical, social inquiry. Unlike training, there is never an end point or the premise of eventually becoming an expert. Ideas and information come not only from listening to others but from interacting with them dialectically.

The team leader lives in a state of *becoming*. The leader is evolving just as the project evolves. Leaders ask themselves about the quality of the project and search for elements that need to be added to the recipe. Instead of micromanaging, the leader is concerned with motivation of the team players. The feedback received is looked upon as grassroots information about how the leader can improve self-learning and make better contributions.

Teams grow when the individuals on the team are encouraged to explore new ideas and directions. Strengths between peers are nurtured and internal support is developed as the team encounters and overcomes obstacles together.

It is up to everyone in schools to ask questions about how we can successfully transform today's schools into quality-led organizations. How do you build them? How are the people in the schools going to be used most effectively? How can we identify our customers? How are teaching and learning going to improve? A rich conversation ought to be initiated at many levels, in many teams in schools to get to core issues. The quality of the final vision of the reinvented school will evolve from individual ideas and collective team reflection—not from the mind of a single team leader, school principal, superintendent, or other educrat.

LIFELONG LEARNERS

Effective leadership is a must in schools. On some occasions, leaders on campus will find themselves on opposite ends of an issue. One team effort that our school undertook, dealt with the issue of Goals 2000 Standards.

The concern was whether or not our school should apply for National Goals 2000 grant money. This issue was presented a few years ago in our School Site Council composed of parents, support staff, teachers, and the principal. Many people thought application for the grant was correct because emphasizing basic standards of instructional achievement would promote a better education for all students in our school. The criteria of measurement would be norm-referenced tests.

On the opposite end of the controversy, some people felt that the establishment of arbitrary standards of measuring improvement by using norm-referenced tests would impede the school reforms that we had already initiated. (We had initiated major staff development training with our leaders to incorporate authentic assessment criteria for our children.)

Individuals took it upon themselves to delve into healthy dialogue and pursue research on the topic. The area of student achievement, always interesting, took on an even livelier existence. Ultimately, we decided not to initiate writing the grant for Goals 2000, based on Dr. Deming's Eleventh Point of Management: "Eliminate numerical quotas."[5] Test score numbers, remember, take into consideration only the numbers, not the quality of the educational program. We thought that measuring our educational progress by using the results of norm-references test data would have been a step backwards.

The importance of this particular dialogue was that a true community of learners and leaders developed during the discourse. We took to heart how schoolpeople who served in a variety of roles, could assume leadership positions and, concurrently, engage in self-learning. Roland Barth, in *Improving Schools from Within*, speaks of how an anthropologist friend told him that "dramatic, profound learning takes place in societies in which people of all ages, generations and positions live work and learn together simultaneously."

Barth finds this to be a "yeasty" environment for learning that is always changing, exploring, and probing.[6] Collective inquiry of issues affecting school life reminds all of the need to continue our learning. If we really are serious about being lifelong learners we must be committed to our own learning. Leaders emerge when they transfer their learning into fresh thinking about school issues.

The best leaders are lifelong learners. The very best practices of educational leaders are learned practices. Learning is renewing. The best schools embody a culture that invites learning. Those in leadership roles in the school frame the learning by supporting ongoing dialogue and building upon the learning of others.

Leaders with a clear vision of their role in the school lead others to new levels of self-learning. When they are a role model for inquiry, creativity, and promoting a vision of the future, others become motivated to engage in self-renewal. The best leaders are excellent learners who effect the changes needed to create quality schools.

LEARNING WINDOW 4.3
A Community of Learners Led by
Many Leaders Is Fostered by

✔ Articulating goals
✔ Relinquishing authority to schoolpeople
✔ Involving schoolpeople before decisions are made
✔ Sharing responsibility for failure
✔ Giving schoolpeople credit for success

Adapted from Roland Barth

TEACHER LEADERS

Teacher leaders are vital to the emerging wisdom of a school culture. One of the major characteristics of quality organizations is that they encourage a high degree of employee participation in decision making. It is no longer a viable option for teachers to choose to close their doors and not participate in the critical issues that affect our schools.

Teachers need to take an active role in shaping the direction of learning, teaching practices, and how the budget is spent. In order for teachers to take responsibility for their professional lives, they should learn as much as possible about all aspects of school life. By becoming more knowledgeable, they will be able to ask the right questions.

In one instance at one of the schools where I served as principal, a teacher asked a question that resulted in a singular experience for many children and adults. At a leadership council this teacher asked if, as part of a culmination of an oceanography unit, it would be possible to take our eldest students on a field trip to San Diego to visit Sea World. After brainstorming the possibilities, subteams were self-selected and began in earnest to research cost, transportation, insurance, parent involvement, and fund-raising. Leaders emerged in these subteams. They worked with others to crystallize goals, identify resources, and establish time lines.

After many months of children and adults selling candy bars and engaging in oceanography lessons supported by the education department at Sea World, the class did, indeed, fly from Los Angeles to San Diego. From there they took a bus from the San Diego airport, paid entrance fees, enjoyed the learning experience, and returned home. This was a school in a very poor neighborhood where, for many of the students, a chance to fly on an airplane and visit Sea World would have to be considered nearly impossible.

This experience was a dramatic step forward for all concerned. It proved that, when people choose to work together because of a compelling desire to achieve a final goal, they can learn to rely on each other to complete the task.

STUDENT LEARNERS

There are many opportunities for students to assume leadership roles at schools. Usually these involve the student council, safeties, or play leaders in elementary schools, but they are more sophisticated in secondary schools. One leadership role that I have introduced at schools where I have served as principal is that of the "conflict manager."

Conflict managers are selected by teachers based on their verbal capabilities, teamwork skills, and leadership talents. They are trained to work in pairs, roving the play yard at recess and lunch, interceding when they see conflicts emerging between fellow students. When they intercede, they do not tell the children they are in trouble or write their names down. Instead, they ask each person to present his or her side of the issue and encourage the disputing parties to engage in dialogue about how to resolve their problem without further escalation.

Needless to say, the conflict manager process is an unqualified success. It has worked so effectively that I've often expressed to parents and staff members what a great world it would be if we had conflict managers roaming our streets to intercede and obtain peaceful solutions for adults who were on the verge of escalating their personal differences.

PARENT AND COMMUNITY LEADERS

School site councils, advisory councils, instructional transition teams and parent teacher organizations offer opportunities for adults to work with staff members to share their insights on how to improve schools. These teams are an invitation for people to move beyond single loop participation in schools such as volunteering in classrooms or baking cookies.

One example of a unique collaboration that was initiated by my Instructional Transition Team a few years ago was a "State of the School Report." Just as the president of the United States annually presents a State of the Union report to the American citizenry, it was determined that our team would be responsible for compiling and presenting a report containing our mission and vision statement, allocation of budget, staff training processes, parent/community involvement and instructional practices that we had implemented during the course of the year.

This team was an exciting amalgamation of talent from the first day. We had open parent meetings for input on some items and presented information at others. The bottom line was that the adults took control over their own learning because they found so much significance in the project.

The final document was printed and distributed to all parents. Furthermore, it was replicated in the neighborhood newspaper and even presented on our local cable television channel. On the television program, each member of the Instructional Transition Team presented a portion of the report and fielded questions initiated by a television reporter and newspaper writer.

SUPPORT STAFF LEADERS

Support staffs, consisting of clerical, custodial, teacher assistants, and yard supervisors are seldom viewed with the same reverence as teachers or parents. I think this is a major oversight. Support staffs are a vital part of the learning community and should be afforded full partnership and have the same opportunities to dialogue about their perceptions on how to improve school life.

Schools should mirror our multicultural, diverse, pluralistic society. We need thinkers from all corners of the school population to help us address the pressing issues of the day. Support staff have the capacity and willingness to tackle difficult issues and resolve them with precision and finality.

I recall one significant effort that emanated from an Advisory Council meeting. It concerned earthquakes, which are always a concern for those of us who live in Southern California. They are a way of life that we tolerate for the privilege of enjoying a wonderful climate.

Many of our support staff members had children in attendance at our school, which caused them to have insights on safety that were not shared

---

ANNALEE AVENUE SCHOOL
Emergency Plan

✔ Students will be evacuated from campus to Carson Park.
✔ Principal and staff will supervise students until they are picked up.
✔ Telephone calls to school will not be acknowledged if we have relocated. We will have telephone access to you if needed.
✔ You may obtain additional information by tuning to:
KNX Radio (1070 AM)
All local television stations
Criteria Cable TV Channel 3

by the rest of us. Leaders from the support staff team designed a plan for evacuation to a local park that did not have building structures, trees, or power lines—which offer the potential for harm in the event of a powerful earthquake. They made the necessary telephone calls to secure permission from the city for evacuation, typed wallet sized cards for the parents that contained emergency information, established drill procedures, updated student emergency cards, and solicited, collected, and stored children's "earthquake packets" consisting of a drink, snacks such as Granola bars, bandages, and flashlights. Other leaders on the team were able to obtain donations from local businesses for additional food supplies for those children who could not financially provide them.

PRINCIPAL LEADERS

Contemporary schools require principals who seek high levels of participation from schoolpeople. They should have a strong vision of a place of embarkation on the journey toward quality. Principals must balance competency with integrity, look beyond numbers to see people, and establish frameworks for schoolpeople to engage in meaningful dialogue about improving practices and processes.

It is also important for principals to take control of their learning. By being leaders of learning, principals can radically reconceptualize their role. Principals need to be ready to learn about circumstances at the school and also about emerging ideas that may help them shape a better school.

One aspect of principal-led learning was initiated by Professor Roland Barth of Harvard University over a decade ago. He helped establish university-sponsored centers for the exchange of "craft knowledge" among principals in a conversational forum. These conversations offer principals a haven in which to express advocacy and learn strategies for transformational, instructional, and administrative improvements. As of the date of the writing of this book, I serve as the president of the U.C.L.A. Principals' Center. We are members of the Harvard University International Network of Principals' Centers, which now flourish throughout our nation and have made significant growth with new charters internationally.

Much of my personal learning has been stimulated in these principal conversations. My studies of TQM, learning organizations, team learning, the power of dialogue, and the metaphysics of quality are all a direct result of conversations at different principal center activities. I have applied this learning in establishing many team formats that are described, at length, in chapter 7. Some of these team enterprises have been published in professional journals and other ideas have appeared in book form.

When the principal of the school assumes the role of "lead learner," exciting possibilities await. The wise principal will understand that there are many leaders at a school. They will be the ones who tap this valuable resource by establishing frameworks whereby people may dialogue in meaningful terms in team learning ventures.

THE SERVANT LEADER

One overlooked aspect of being a team leader is a basic prerequisite for leaders in any quality enterprise: a responsibility to identify and groom potential leaders for new teams. Leaders should target people who have a range and depth, who celebrate the human spirit and have an optimistic, glowing vision of what schools may become. They should look for people who construct meaning from each experience, achieve success while defying convention, and create new knowledge in interactive team audiences.

The most effective team leaders create, share, and embrace new ideas. They identify opportunities and engage others in linking opportunities to effective change. They are flexible and adapt to feedback from the team. They understand that the team develops a life of its own. When rocky times come, a disequilibrium may actually strengthen the team. They know enough about the nature of teams to let the disequilibrium run its course.

In nature, it is common knowledge that disequilibrium is a part of the evolutionary growth process. Nature does not demand perfection in this process, only growth. When human beings in an organization interface, there is no demand for perfection, but a hopeful prospect for growth.

Servant leaders encourage and accept change and growth. They view and evaluate the organization as a whole system. Leaders recognize the collective power and energy that teams possess. Each leader understands that the creation of a reinvented school requires that people look to reinvent themselves. They acknowledge that the act of reinvention is a good thing.

Servant leaders are always trying to solve issues. They know that teams seriously outperform individuals. Paradoxically, they also understand that you must have individuals coming together to form a team. Wise leaders also know that each person possesses an evolving craft knowledge consisting of small wisdoms accumulated through years of practice When teams synergize, these small wisdoms can become grand messages and create a path of action to accomplish goals.

Most of all servant leaders enjoy the journey that probes the uncharted depths of their own hearts and minds. They are not dismayed with ambiguity. It is all right not to know everything. It is proper to explore and reflect. When we find out what we are afraid of, we find out what we are made of.

The language spoken in teams gives service to the art of team leadership. Leaders gain insights on the human condition and how the story of each school is driven by the characters who work in close proximity with the students. They inspire schoolpeople to move beyond visceral complaints and on to collaboration to face and resolve the issues of the day. They even encourage a postproduction of these collaborations by ensuring that others are prompted to assume future team leadership roles and pass on knowledge and resources to future teams.

Effective team leadership is a product of strong leadership from school administrators who employ TQM and learning organization principles and practices in their schools. It is an enduring testament to the school administration that teams are able to make important decisions affecting school life. The intrinsic desire of people to improve the school environment is reinforced when they are accepted as full partners in the decision-making processes instead of being given some synthetic, subtext role to play on an advisory board that never addresses important issues.

Rivers run in one direction. Teams learn to flow with their own success. When teams find they possess a strength in their unity and can traverse difficult terrain, they pick up velocity and increase their capacity

---

LEARNING WINDOW 4.4
Stem Questions to See What Learning
Is Taking Place at Your School

✔ How do we develop a community of learners? How do we create a school with many leaders?
✔ How can leaders promote dialogue among teachers, paraprofessionals, support staff, parents, students, and other schoolpeople?
✔ How can we ask schoolpeople to seek out higher standards for their personal learning without imposing standardization?
✔ How is accountability fostered in team learning?

and capability for change. Furthermore, they increase the capability of the entire school culture to embrace change. I have witnessed, firsthand, the dramatic growth in school cultures where I have served as principal when teams have been able to unleash their full potential to solve issues regarding the improvement of teaching and learning practices.

The servant leader has a consummate need to absorb knowledge and provoke change. However, it is the wisdom of teams that insists that change be transformed from energy of the mind to actual implementation. School life, consisting of bell schedules, accumulation of disparate subject matter, and other systematic routines, should not be a series of spaces to be measured for the day. The human brain craves open spaces for exploring new knowledge. Teams offer individuals an opportunity to showcase their ability and talent. Leaders promote enterprises that give people in the culture an opportunity to prove their substance. Schoolpeople have a story to tell. Only they can change the boundaries of vision and reality. The servant leader has a wisdom to value the burning collective intelligence of people. They understand the need to develop a united purpose to achieve quality.

ENDNOTES

1. Cresencio Torres, *The Tao of Teams* (San Diego: Pfeiffer and Company, 1994).
2. Peter Scholtes, *The Team Handbook: How to Use Teams to Improve Quality* (Madison, WI: Joiner and Associates, 1989).
3. Lee G. Bolman, *Leading with Soul* (San Francisco: Jossey-Bass, 1996).
4. Cresencio Torres, *The Tao of Teams* (San Diego: Pfeiffer and Company, 1994).
5. Mary Walton, *The Deming Management Method* (New York: Perigree Books, 1986). From The Deming Management Method "Fourteen Points."
6. Roland Barth, *Improving Schools from Within: Teachers, Parents and Principals Can Make the Difference* (San Francisco: Jossey-Bass, 1991).

LEARNING WINDOW

4.3 Roland Barth, *Improving Schools from Within: Teachers, Parents and Principals Can Make the Difference* (San Francisco: Jossey-Bass, 1991).

CHAPTER

Reflective
Practice

"Toto, I've a feeling we're not in Kansas anymore!"

—Dorothy, The Wizard of Oz

We are only now beginning to understand aspects of modern management systems. It is essential that the Western style of management, which has been successful in the past, change. This is true in our schools as well as in American industry. The perplexing issue for everyone is "how" to implement the changes necessary in our schools.

In our contemporary world, which emphasizes congruent relationships, organizations would do well to design work practices that cultivate a partnership between people and the system for which they work. TQM is a forerunner in meeting organizational behavior needs by creating the possibilities of developing a trusting network between management and the workforce. By recognizing the talents of people, TQM helps create bonds among people where adversarial rifts may have existed before.

TQM is all about teamwork and the possibilities of team learning; it offers a new way for schools to do business. Leaders in schools must address the transformation effort, and to do so, they have to change their traditional roles and acquire new skills. Most of all they must see the potential of active leadership and participation from all aspects of the school environment. Quality is something that cannot be delegated. Active leadership produces the amalgamated benefit of having people at all levels become vital resources to resolve problems or improve processes in team fashion.

Schoolpeople need to create dramatic change in the way they have been doing business. If schoolpeople do not hear this message, the public school system in our nation will suffer and the children will lose.

Schools are tradition-bound archetypes that are modeled along stratified, bureaucratic lines from another era in our country. "Critics and scholars argue that traditional theories of leadership in schools are no longer valid because practical realities demand new frameworks." Yet we continue to "see evidence that elements of . . . traditional thinking survive" in educational administration thinking.[1]

Meanwhile, teachers remain isolated from one another, and therefore, incapacitated in any attempt to acquire new information about how to improve teaching practices or share information with colleagues about how to become more knowledgeable in their profession. Furthermore, they impart fragmented bits of knowledge to students in 50-minute blocks of time about math, social studies, and the like, and leave the youngsters to their own devices to make sense of it.

Implementing collective learning processes would appear to be a way to end this recurring bad dream. It is also a means to "enhance collaborative, caring leadership."[2] Teams are a cornerstone for articulation and reflection on how to best prepare students for a future world that will change by the nanosecond.

When schoolpeople model participation in learning processes, they, as a starting point, influence students to understand the importance of becoming lifelong learners. By participating in team enterprises, schoolpeople emerge from narrow frameworks and learn the benefits of a broad, free range of references. It is the practice of team learning that offers schoolpeople some hope.

Teams, while only a part of the quality management principle and practice package, offer formidable mechanisms to help resuscitate our schools. Quality alliances contribute to interaction and upgrade the capacity for people to generate ideas for improvement. Teams of schoolpeople, in a variety of possible alignments, serve to round the corners and smooth over the rough edges of the static, bureaucratic order. Brisk dialogue within these teams reawakens the human capacity to thoroughly probe new horizons of thought.

As long as schools remain where they always have been, they will never realize the true value of team alliances, let alone ever access the potential of becoming a part of the quality movement.

TEAMS AT WORK

Team members are usually selected by someone at the school who serves in a formal leadership capacity. However, there may be times when individuals are selected by a team leader. It is the nature of the project that is

LEARNING WINDOW 5.1
Effective Team Learning Principles

✔ Listen rather than debate.
✔ Look for opportunities to summarize and ask questions to make sure there is agreement and understanding.
✔ Don't digress, stay with the agenda.
✔ Remind team members of deadlines.
✔ Look for consensus.
✔ Evaluate each team meeting either with a formal, written evaluation or verbal feedback to ensure that future meetings will be productive.

Adapted from Peter Scholtes

usually the determining factor in identifying them. As a rule, the more knowledge they have about the content of the project, the more they are likely to reap benefits from its results, and the more likely they are to serve on the team.

Team members, whether they are the teaching faculty, support staff, community people, parents, or students should seize the opportunity to share their insights and learn from others in teams. A key to learning organization disciplines is that people must be allowed to participate in ongoing, powerful communication. Members should come to understand that their attendance at meetings, service on subteams, and doing follow-up work is vital to the success of the team. An individual's talents and expertise have to be shared with others in this venture, which may include work outside the normal realm of team meetings.

Team members become productive participants by following the previously cited techniques of effective dialogues and attentive listening. Every meeting should include opportunities for team members to have extended conversations regarding various aspects of the project. The more time spent on clarification of purpose or explanation of proposals, the more effective the team will be in pursuing its objectives.

Compatible teams benefit from team efforts in keeping all parties on track. When everyone pulls together, the final product is richer. When teams are constantly engaged in upgrading their work processes, they work through any thoughts of deviation, which wastes time and energy.

High-powered teams are flexible, make immediate corrections when potential problems arise, and solve problems as an entire team.

The following Team Meeting Record and Team Meeting Evaluation are forms that I devised as a school principal and may prove to be of value for schoolpeople interested in optimizing the effectiveness of their meetings.

TEAM MEETING RECORD

SCHOOL TEAM _____

Meeting Number _____   Date _____   Place _____
Goals of Team Project _____

_____

_____

AGENDA

Topic	Person(s) to Lead	Minutes Allocated
◆ Ice Breaker	Ruth	3
◆		
◆		
◆		
◆ Set Agenda/Date for Next Meeting	Bill	1
◆ Review of Meeting	Caren	5

FOLLOW-UP

Goals Champions

◆
◆

IDEA BIN

Items for Future Conversations

◆
◆

TEAM MEETING EVALUATION

Meeting Number _____   Date _____   By Name (Optional) _____

I Expected _____

_____

_____

_____

_____

_____

I Got _____

_____

_____

_____

_____

_____

I Valued _____

_____

_____

_____

_____

_____

I Would Like _____

_____

_____

_____

_____

_____

LEARNING TOGETHER

Roland Barth is fond of relating an experience he had as a principal of an elementary school. Several years ago, he held a faculty meeting and was puzzled by the catatonic stupor of the teachers in attendance. Whenever he tried to open things up for interaction, he was greeted with dead silence. After the meeting, he chanced to walk near a hallway where many of the teachers had congregated.

They were having a rousing conversation about the school issues they felt were important. Dr. Barth contemplated how to transfer this hallway conversation to formal, school-sponsored meetings. It was from this revelation that the premise for the Principals' Center Conversations format was born.

All principals have experienced the phenomenon related by Dr. Barth. We know schoolpeople want to talk about the things they feel are really important, and every school principal has asked himself or herself how to harness this inquisitive energy source.

Creating a framework for self-initiated, reflective learning at the school has been a consuming passion for me as well. Specific examples of actual practice are enumerated in chapter 7, but first it is important to explore the psychology of this desire for schoolpeople to share, reflect, and learn together.

Conversing is the primary mode in which school teams work together. A stabilizing factor in assisting teams to achieve quality results is the development of a common goal for the project they are entrusted with completing. Team members need an opportunity, at the initial meeting, to talk about how the project will unfold, based on a common understanding of the goal to be achieved. From initial encounters, planning begins in earnest. Leadership roles within the team are established, data gathered, members learn to resolve personal differences, resources are identified, and the capacity to foster leadership in others is developed.

The more people have an opportunity to meet to dialogue, the better the team's chances are of being successful. Teams create their personalized map to chart how things will be accomplished as they build relationships and team skills. It is a good idea to foster openness at initial meetings as much as possible when deciding on a course of action for a project. By probing a full range of reference, participants build a capacity for team and self-learning.

Teams that talk together work well together. Those that do not have the opportunity for open dialogue invariably are crippled. One person or another takes control of the team for his or her own purposes, people become protective of ideas and are unwilling to share, turf becomes an issue, or anxiety about deadlines leads to other conflicting undercurrents. To attempt to revive such teams once this level of distrust is present is extremely difficult.

Open dialogue attracts ideas. Ideas spark insights, build unity for goals, and promotes lasting learning. Learning engages the entire physiology: Our bodies function better, we are more alert, our body may tilt gently forward, we are more attuned listeners, and we become more aware than usual of our surroundings and inner passions when we are part of a lively discourse.

Team learning encourages a vibrancy of exuberant social and intellectual interaction. The clarity of voicing ideas invites others into the circle. A bright partnership is born in this environment that reshapes boundaries and creates and refines new forms and structures of collaboration. The social energy of teams cuts across layers of bureaucracy to create seamless lines of interaction. The fabric woven from team learning is stronger than the most polished sculpture and softer than the most exquisite silk.

When teams learn together they promote relationships that encourage people to look forward, not backward. Trust in the team promotes risk taking instead of being drowned in overanalysis. Teams clarify group learning by encouraging individuals the opportunity to frame their own reflective learning. At the core of self-learning is individual reflection on ideas that have been shared. If we want to get the school to change, we need people to reflect on their learning and make application of the learning daily. Teaching and learning practices change when people contemplate their own learning and put it to use.

The very best school teams galvanize a commitment to growth and success for everyone on the team. When all are pulling together they achieve peak efficiency. A common focus fosters mutual accountability. Interdependence lends to productive work. The entire team endeavor moves through four distinct stages of unsentimental evolution:

Stage One: FORMING
This is a transition stage from individual to team member status. As teams form, members cautiously explore acceptable boundaries. Individuals learn to find resources from within the group in this stage.

- Group behaviors are polite and cautious.
- Roles on the team are ambiguous.
- An orientation process commences, providing a net for team members to test boundaries, build foundations for trust, and explore group behavior.
- Abstract dialogue takes place regarding project issues.

Stage Two: STORMING

This is far and away the most stressful stage in team building. Impatience may lead to internal struggles about the correct path to take to complete the project. Some people may become so disenchanted with the process that they remove themselves from participatory roles in the team and decide to march onward with their own agendas. Because so few members have a knowledge base for the value of TQM team enterprises, much of their energy is devoted to resistance and blaming others instead of focusing on the work to be done.

- Teams lack experience working together.
- Individuals rely on their own skills and resources at times.
- Struggles develop about the best course of action to take to accomplish goals.
- The ship begins to "righten" as leadership tasks begin to be shared by team members.
- Patterns develop for working together and developing a common purpose.
- Conversations focus on the direction that the team should take.
- Attention moves from blaming others to focusing on what the team is doing right.

Stage Three: NORMING

Team members become more accepting of the team concept. They begin to see the value of synergizing and tapping the talent pool that exist within the team. Harmony replaces conflict in this stage. Individual team members begin to concentrate more on their part of the project resulting in significant progress being accomplished.

- Conversations build levels of trust, promote honesty and valuing others.
- A sense of team cohesion develops.
- Members work through their differences.
- The team picks up productivity.

LEARNING WINDOW 5.2

Acknowledging Strengths Within the Team

- ✔ Valuing of interdependence.
- ✔ Self-initiating.
- ✔ High degree of self-learning.
- ✔ Ethereal conversations.
- ✔ High trust.
- ✔ High performance.

From Bruce Tuckeman

Stage Four: PERFORMING
At this stage, the team is performing at optimum capacity. Issues are resolved quickly. The focus is on solving problems so that the team can address the core project. Team members freely acknowledge and access strengths that exist from within.

To reiterate, teams only get better with practice. To achieve ultimate proficiency, they must "work" through the four stages, refining processes and learning from one another along the way. As a process, the four stages are not dissimilar to the Shewhart/Deming PLAN-DO-STUDY-ACT Cycle that is fundamental to any quality management enterprise.

PRIVILEGED TOURISTS

At the forming stage of team building, members enter as privileged tourists. They are poised between belief and disbelief, uncertain about the prospects of performing in a team and not clear what their roles will be. There may be some degree of hopefulness, but this can be dispelled rather quickly in the storming stage.

Teams grow as they work together, clarify team goals, learn to define roles, identify internal strengths and weaknesses, anticipate problems, and achieve success. Do not doubt for a single instant that success breeds future success. It changes the personality of a team member from a tourist to an active, vital participant in a winning collaboration. The glue that holds people together so they can stretch and grow is founded in extensive dialogue opportunities that fuel successful team collaborations.

Dialogue changes the mind-set of individuals. Those who come aboard thinking they are going to partake of an expensive lunch cannot remain neutral or unaffected by serious team inquiry. Teams pull individuals in by tapping the soul of the human spirit. To be validated by colleagues as well as to achieve some level of independent learning is at the core of transformational reflective learning. In many instances, people who enter teams as tourists, evolve as full-fledged team players at the completion of the project.

Team projects offer an opportunity for liberation. People keep changing personal and organizational boundaries, redefining old ways and transforming school into something special. The team enterprise is a far easier thing to experience than to write about. The human brain is processing so many things simultaneously that words fail to do justice to the enterprise. Team learning is a multidimensional experience that no mere written description can adequately explain.

THE SOCIAL INTELLIGENCE OF DIALOGUE

There are tens of thousands of school districts in the United States and it is difficult to attempt reconstruction of so many tradition-bound institutions. It is probably best to attempt to concentrate renewal energies one school at a time. Systemic restructuring practices in school districts have either been dismal failures or half-hearted tries by well-intentioned people. Instead of exhausting valuable energy attempting to change vast institutionalized inertia from hundreds of years, it may be best to attempt to erect powerful teams on small fertile fields at school sites where we can cultivate the crops of self-renewal and lifelong learning.

Each team and each team member is part of an uplifting learning ensemble. They learn from one another by sharing craft knowledge that occupies the majority of space of team conversations. Schoolpeople cross new borders, break from old patterns of behavior, and provoke fellow team members to reflect about the value of old assumptions and icons in team learning. True restructuring of schools cannot ever really take place when mandated from above—the superintendent or board-member level. Only the powerful human resources that exist at each school can successfully reposition people. The wisdom of teams to shape new avenues of thinking, envision the possible, and improve student achievement is the product of high-performance teams.

Deep dialogue encourages mobilization and movement toward team goals. This dialogue is a social construction that invites team members to become increasingly connected to all the other players. As they learn to communicate effectively, teams develop a sense of control over the learning process and their own destiny.

The language of teams expands as incentives for ongoing learning are encouraged. High levels of thinking are expected in a culture that pushes for enlightenment. Each person is capable of adding to the mix of important idea development. Dialogue experiences offer a unique bridge for individuals to progress from the unknown to the known and back again.

THE POWER OF DIALOGUE IN CREATING A COMMUNITY OF LEARNERS

School life is very fragmented. There are bell schedules, nutrition breaks, lunch schedules, times set aside for assemblies, faculty meeting times, and, in secondary schools, arbitrary periods for subject matter. Furthermore, subject matter is taught in fragments, for the most part, in our

American school system today. Teachers interact in fragmented mini-speak sessions between classes. We test student knowledge based on fragments of memorized factoids and we go home to a fragmented lifestyle.

As a result, teachers and students tend to think in fragmented pieces. In secondary schools, moreso than elementary, there are many artificial departments, compartments, and multiple lines of authority that further splinter the school community and prove to be counterproductive to the school culture. With our schools divided into bits and pieces, there is no wonder that they appear to be drifting toward an atmosphere of incoherence.

Schools have become separate and unequal. There is no common understanding when relationships are not promoted. From the outside and inside, schools appear to be a mix of poorly related parts carved into pieces that lack cohesive meaning. This is the same phenomenon that Robert Pirsig, author of the previously mentioned *Zen and the Art of Motorcycle Maintenance*, warns us about.[3]

Fragmentation is dangerous in that it produces minds that fall into an institutional groove. Specialized functions do not add to a depth of understanding within the school culture, but rather, cloud the school vision. "Rather than reason together, people defend their parts."[4] When people become defensive about their work situations, there is little hope that they will break bread together in the spirit of creating a higher level of team wisdom.

No wonder schools appear to be stuck in the same place, year after year. It is only when schoolpeople join together in productive dialogue about how to improve schools that real change transpires. Fragmentation causes polarization. People feel they are constrained and not appreciated for their contributions in a nontrusting environment. They are not given time to reflect on their practice. Consequently, people don't have an opportunity to self-evaluate and change.

When schoolpeople are encouraged to inquire collectively, they can confront their performance and move on to higher ground. Purposeful dialogue will surface only when people in the school culture come to realize how they fit in the broad scheme of things. If they recognize that there is an intention of understanding and support within a collegial team, they will talk about important issues. Unity and relationships that materialize over the course of team dialogue tend to close off opportunities for a clashing of viewpoints.

The quality and level of inquiry reflects the degree of trust and understanding that has developed among the members of the team. The actual process of team dialogue is one that takes time. Sponsorship of team conversations by school leaders is mandatory if schools are to assume that

```
┌─────────────────────────────────────────────────────┐
│                  LEARNING WINDOW 5.3                  │
│                     Collaboration                     │
│                                                       │
│  ✔ Many organizations look only at parts of people.  │
│  ✔ Quality organizations look at the entire person.  │
│  ✔ Relationships count more than structure.          │
│  ✔ Participative management arises from the heart and │
│    from a personal philosophy about the values of people. │
│                                                       │
│  Adapted from Max DePree (1989)                       │
└─────────────────────────────────────────────────────┘
```

they have any likelihood of creating lasting change. Reflective dialogue is definitely something new. School administrators may have had training in participatory management during university credentialization courses, but this is a horse of a different color.

The dynamics of diversity of thought lead to creative approaches to problem solving and completion of team projects. Unproductive schools exist because people feel they are operating within a restricted margin. When people no longer feel constrained, they tend to become more involved in increasing productivity. When encouraged to participate in a pool of common talent, they rise to the occasion. Learning communities capture a "wholeness" of the culture. When people are able to frame their own interactions and collectively explore new learning, they take ownership of processes, which has a direct correlation to the quality of the outcomes.

When teachers, support staff, or other members of the school culture speak of a lack of communication, they typically point in the direction of the school principal. One of the supreme fallacies of pointing one's finger at anyone is that the bottom three fingers point back at the person doing the pointing! Moreover, finger pointing never uncovers the real problems in any situation and only deepens mistrust. When people feel a lack of direction, they will round up the usual suspects, one of whom is always the school principal. It is almost an unconscious act in some schools and, in most cases, singles out the wrong person at the wrong time.

In schools that operate as a community, every person feels an equal responsibility for all aspects of school life. If the school is foundering, it is because team expectations have not been fulfilled. If the school is moving forward, it is because school teams are meshing in a rhythm of profound understanding, awakening a collective conscious to achieve a quality operation.

> **LEARNING WINDOW 5.4**
> Basic Premises to Promote Reflective Practice
>
> ✔ Suspend assumptions.
> ✔ Listen attentively.
> ✔ Seize opportunities to broaden one's point of view.
> ✔ Find commonalities, make connections.
> ✔ Promote intrinsic motivation.
> ✔ Reason together.

SABOTEURS

Every organization has saboteurs. There will always be people in schools who will resist change, and just because individuals are on a team does not necessarily ensure that they will be team players. If a team gets bogged down by the antics of a single person, it is useful to have the entire team do some soul-searching. Ask members to think about all the disadvantages of disbanding the team, reconvening, and going back to square one. All the good work that has been accomplished by so many people should not be lost due to the sabotage efforts of one wet blanket.

A follow-up step would be to break a large team, down into small units, and brainstorm all the positive processes that have transpired. Have the team focus on the good relationships that have developed, as well as the emerging synergy.

If change in a school is to become a reality, the energy and positive network that have developed must be nurtured. Effective teams are bonded relationships that can deal effectively with differences. People learn to think and speak of connections when they recall team enterprises. If people are encouraged to keep an open mind and are granted opportunities to participate in free-flowing dialogue, there will be fewer detractors, and different points of view will be more accepted.

It is part of our human conditioning to assume that motives exist to explain the behavior of others. Whether we like to admit it or not, we subconsciously judge people in terms of what may be "right" for ourselves. This judgment process is also a part of our efforts to maintain and preserve our own integrity. The team leader and team members can do their part to bring everyone into the fold by making sure that all contributions are validated. The best team members make the most of every situation. By focusing on interpersonal relationships at the outset, affirming contributions, matching the right people with the right team, and representing themselves as always approachable, team leaders can keep the team in self-solvent territory.

Negative sanctions almost never need to be addressed. The caring, inclusive desire of team members to converge on issues rather than personalities is always the proper approach. To act in a trusting manner is a strength; it leads to creativity, productivity, and openness about achieving goals.

Sometimes people appear to be contrary or aloof when it is really their personal style rather than any attempt on their part to debilitate the goals and processes of the team. The most important element to consider in situations where there is anxiety or concerns about sabotage is to keep the conversations going. Suspicions sometimes nurture a darker sort of quiet among people. If team members do not address their concerns, a "freezing" of team momentum may happen. Dialogue may serve to advance opportunities for clarification.

Compassion for divergent points of view ought to mesh with a logical, fair access to the issues at hand. When in doubt as to whether someone is being purposefully obstructive, it is always best to rely on ground rules and look at the message rather than the messenger. Team processes should be "enabling mechanisms" that create an atmosphere in which everyone has a voice. It is true that, on occasion, an independent or contrary voice can lead the majority of the team to reassess their lines of thought. This is the value of self-reflection on ideas presented in team dialogue. Each idea presented may have merit. The ideas only need time for incubation and reflection.

Productive teams learn to probe. They are receptive, empathetic, and interpretive. Their strength lies in the premise that they do not hoard ideas; instead they make sure they market them! Divergent thinking should not be a threat to a viable team. Teams ought to be heuristic models in action—all about discovery for the team and for the self.

When members share the same ideals about the purpose of teams, they interact and plan strategies that reaffirm the value of the team and their individual roles. Trust and connectedness are an invitation to mutual learning and validate personal worth. When schoolpeople invent new knowledge, they tend to reinvent themselves.

SIX POINTS OF TEAM LEARNING

In conveying aspects of team practice it is hard to single out precise, optimum features that may be of specific value to a diverse reading audience.

The attempt to put one's finger on the pulse of team learning is elusive enough, even for individuals who operate in similar contexts. This is because team learning and individual learning are so intertwined. One cannot attempt to keep one eye on the team community while maintaining one eye on the parameters of one's own life. The two should blend with an overlapping focus.

The following six points of team learning have a hybrid quality about them. Some are part of W. Edwards Deming's charter points of management, others are offered by Peter Scholtes and Fred Pryor in their research. They are interrelated and based on experience. It is difficult to think of one aspect without realizing the connections with other points, and it is easy to see how they can be adapted to school life.

One: CONTINUOUS IMPROVEMENT
One of Dr. Deming's charter points of management, continuous improvement, addresses the team need to devise a plan of action to guide the team in adhering to timeliness, schedules, and deadlines, and also to identify possible resources before beginning to embark on the project. By "font-loading" the plan, teams establish basic steps toward continuous improvement of the final product.

Two: COMMUNICATION
Effective team dialogue offers relevant examination of the issue in an environment of free-flowing ideas. Active listening is an important skill to ensure that all information is shared, opportunities for inquiry are provided, and significant contributions are acknowledged. Dialogue serves as a bridge to discoveries of new landscapes in the school community.

Three: TEAM PRACTICE
Mutually agreed upon team behaviors make meetings more productive. Adherence to the agenda, focused inquiries, attentive listening, reframing, and summarizing important points all lead to team success.

Four: DECISION MAKING
You can tell a great deal about a team by observing its decision-making process. Teams can use brainstorming, lateral processing, or analytical approaches, but all ideas require input, inquiry, and reflection before they achieve collaborative acceptance and consensus.

Five: TEAM PROCESS
Team processing is concerned with how efficiently the team is working together. Are deadlines being met? Is everyone on the same page in the team vision? Is there a general agreement on how to intervene to correct problems? Is the team leader meeting everyone's needs?

Six: PROBLEM SOLVING
It is easy to make decisions. It is more difficult to make quality decisions. It is important that teams look for root causation of problems when addressing

needs to be met in their project. Uncovering root issues requires extensive study of quantitative and qualitative data and deep conversations about issues at the core of the school organization. Permanent solutions to problems, rather than quick fixes, are sought.[5]

REFLECTION AND QUALITY

Working in teams addresses primary efficacy issues for schoolpeople. When people come together to collaborate in teams, they speak a common language and learn to value a common vision. For teachers who serve on them, teams offer the prospect of connecting in new ways with colleagues. Under the usual isolated conditions, school life leads them away from one another, pursuing "entirely disparate directions, each teacher compelled by her or his own pedagogical interests, each protected by school norms. . . . Ironically, as teachers contemplate the enormous challenges before them, . . . perhaps the best weapon they could weld against uncertainty lies in colleagues, particularly teacher leaders, within their schools."[6]

Quality schools place a large stock in quality teams. They have outstanding educational leadership, active involvement from schoolpeople, a vision of quality, belief that all students will achieve, and ongoing dialogues about improving teaching and learning. Teams learn to stretch their vision by achieving success in projects.

Team learning authenticates the value of schoolpeople as they merge energies, searching for depth and detail about complex issues. Irresistible and exuberant ideas come from everywhere and everyone in smart teams. The language of the teams is spirited and important. Reflective dialogue renders, for schoolpeople bent on transformation change, clear service to their art and practice.

As people participate in dialogue, they soon learn that the process is not about changing the minds of others so much as learning about chang-

---

LEARNING WINDOW 5.5

"Keep people in the dark and the organization stays in the dark ages. Let in the light, and people can see where they are going."

—*William A. Pasmore*

ing oneself. In reflection, people move to higher levels of self-discovery. We are the cycle we want to improve.

It is easy to become intoxicated by the romance and freedom of reflective dialogue. It is a vehicle for self-transformation. Dialogue leads us on a path toward personal continuous, critical, social inquiry and self-renewal.

Team reflective practice optimizes the uncovering of fresh knowledge from all potential sources in the educational community. When team members are brought together to dialogue, human imagination has no boundaries. To make the music of thoughtful conversations, every person engages in the deft practice of appreciating the shapes and sounds of the words as though they were notes in a symphony. When people share their perceptions and tap into the learning of others, they learn to interpret the phrasing and savor the space between the notes of the message. The more opportunities that team players have to come together to practice the cords and intertwine in a clear harmony with the other members of the dialogue orchestra, the more they stretch their own learning experience. Reflective practice beckons those who would like to take the first step in a long process toward composing the collaborative songs of lifelong learning. And to compose these songs of lifelong learning, one needs to take the risk of speaking the first note.

The ancient Greeks placed reasoning ability on a higher plateau than quality. This preference for science over human judgment has proliferated over the ages and is a mainstay in our contemporary world. Consequently, we tend to do what is reasonable rather than attempt to produce quality. In our world, Americans fervently worship technology and machinery over nature. There appears to be a common-sense, proper way to do things, which schools relish. This is a cause for concern among disciples of W. Edwards Deming and the quality movement. Quality is an open system. Quality defies being measured in absolute terms.

LEARNING WINDOW 5.6

"The teacher's isolation in her classroom works against reflection-in-action. She needs to communicate her private puzzles and insights, to test them against the views of her peers."

—*Donald A. Schon*

Reflection offers a kind of openness we need in schools if we are to hear each other at all. The heart, according to the French, has its places that reason cannot touch. If we open our hearts and minds to the words of our colleagues, we can become more enlightened leaders. We can chart our course through the swift rapids of change and discover new places of learning.

When schoolpeople embrace quality experiences like team reflective dialogue, they move to a higher, uncommon ground. Team learning is a warm place—warmed by the kindred spirit of human energy. And while the team members may be familiar to the eye, the direction of the conversation may take the players to an uncommon ground. An enthusiasm within each person serves to drive the total experience. The road to quality begins with the spoken word.

SUSPENDED CERTAINTY

Whether or not you are a fan of modern abstract art, we all have had the experience of gazing at an abstract painting assuming that recognizable forms are hidden therein. This is because our brains are always seeking out patterns.

When we allow ourselves to suspend the certainty that such forms are there, waiting for us to detect them, we realize that we are no longer prisoners of looking at the painting. Instead, we are looking *through it*, discovering associations and networks of relationships. Similarly, when we suspend our assumptions about how learning has traditionally taken place for schoolpeople in the past—largely through staff development—we free ourselves from self-inflicted boxes.

Learning can take place in a variety of situations for schoolpeople. We need only to create the framework and atmosphere for trust in schools for the learning to flourish. When we reflect on our practice, as educators, we grasp the possibilities of changing what we are doing to improve teaching and learning.

An aesthetic learning curve exists in all good team communication. The more people practice the art of reflective dialogue, the more adroit they become at skillful listening and reflective practice. For example, learning sessions about how to improve teaching practices involve everyone on the team in creating personal mental imagery about the words they hear and in contemplating some level of self-evaluation about how they could improve their own practice in the classroom.

Reflection calls for true soul-searching. As individuals engage in a journey about self-truth, they uncover personal blind spots about their

---

LEARNING WINDOW 5.7
Stem Questions to Promote
Reflective Practice in Your School

✔ What opportunities presently exist in our school for
people to reflect on their practices? How can they be
enhanced? Expanded?
✔ Robert Pirsig warns us about the parts becoming more
important than the whole. How can we break
institutional pieces at school, such as departments,
fragmented 50-minute blocks of instruction and
teaching facts, to appreciating the whole educational
enterprise?
✔ How does reflective practice validate that TQM is an
open system?

---

own failings. They also come to see self-imposed limitations. The renaissance experience for a reflective practitioner transpires when he or she comes to realize a fulfilled promise to become a productive, creative lifelong learner.

ENDNOTES

1. Catherine Marshall, J. Patterson, D. Rogers, and J. Steele, "Caring as a Career: An Alternative Perspective for Educational Administration," *Educational Administration Quarterly* 32 No. 2 (April 1996).
2. N. Noddings, *The Challenge to Care in Schools: An Alternative Approach to Education* (New York: Teachers College Press, 1992).
3. Robert M. Pirsig, *Zen and the Art of Motorcycle Maintenance: An Inquiry into Values* (New York: Morrow and Company, 1974).
4. William Isaacs, "Dialogue: The Power of Collective Thinking," in Kellie T. Wardman, ed., *Reflections on Creating Learning Organizations* (Cambridge, MA: Pegasus Communications, 1994).
5. Much of the information shared in the six points emanates from Peter R. Scholtes, *The Team Handbook* (Madison, WI: Joiner and Associates, 1989); W. Edwards Deming, *Out of the Crisis*

(Cambridge, MA; M.I.T. Center for Advanced Engineering Study, 1986); and Fred Pryor, *The Energetic Manager* (Englewood Cliffs, NJ: Prentice-Hall, 1987).

6. S. Rosenholtz, *Teacher's Workplace: The Social Organization of Schools* (New York: Longman, 1989).

LEARNING WINDOWS

5.1 Some ideas from this list are taken from Peter R. Scholtes, et al., *The Team Handbook: How to Use Teams to Improve Quality* (Madison, WI: Joiner Associates, 1989).

5.2 Most of this material has been extrapolated from Bruce Tuckeman, "Development Sequence in Small Groups," *Psychological Bulletin* 1 (1955).

5.3 Max DePree, *Leadership as an Art* (New York: Doubleday, 1989).

5.5 William A. Pasmore, *Creating Strategic Change: Designing the Flexible, High-Performing Organization* (New York: John Wiley and Sons, Inc., 1994).

5.6 Donald A. Schon, *The Reflective Practitioner: How Professionals Think in Action* (New York: Basic Books, 1983).

CHAPTER

How Learning Organizations Maximize People's Talents

"There exists in man's soul an element that is original to him and personal, and not merely the consequence of society's influence. This aspect of man's should sometimes strike out toward absolute and unconditioned truth."

—*Martin Buber*

If we desire to have quality schools we must ensure that schoolpeople have the occasion to display their unique talents in crafting strategies and structuring new alliances. Schoolpeople should recognize their changing roles at the school site, as well as how their contributions embellish the overall school vision. The school game has changed. Educators should be more cognizant of attempting to meet customer needs. We should pull people in to ask important questions about improving schools. As they reflect on school issues, it will become important that they not only learn to work together to solve problems, but also use their communication and reflective skills to "recognize" problems.

Learning organizations place a new focus on peoples' work. The premise of the learning organization movement is to improve successions of internal processes that will translate into higher quality. So, too, is it a basic tenet of TQM that the people closest to the work need to take responsibility for solving problems and creating innovative practices to improve it. People cannot be taken for granted in a total quality culture. Hence, learning organizations and quality organizations have a similar focus on the intrinsic value of people. Both about people learning to maximize their professional performance.

Extended passages for learning have to be constructed so that schoolpeople can demystify old barriers that prevented open, team communication with one another. By being part of significant teams they learn to make timely, quality decisions about important issues affecting school life. The deep understanding of one's work is possible only when people have an opportunity to participate in team enterprises that extoll the virtues of what Dr. Deming referred to as "optimizing the system."

Optimizing the system calls for active learning. This active learning best takes place in teams that promote dialogue and reflection, therefore allowing each person a window to construct personal meaning in the organization by recognizing patterns, synthesizing disparate information, and constructing solutions. One's effectiveness at work depends on how much support exists within the make-up of the team to promote new learning and self-efficacy.

The construction of "new knowledge" is the most important resource in the learning organization.[1] Creating high-performance innovations, breaking traditional rules, and sponsoring forums for influential thinking opportunities demand a great deal of time. Achieving new knowledge is a slow process. It is a truism that many adults in our modern society construct their learning more slowly than skyscrapers are built. People need to interpret and reflect on how new information or processes affect their everyday lives. Serious shifts in thinking take time.

The wherewithal for schools to achieve quality may rest with schoolpeople who can come to view the school as an organizational system that expects changes and improvements. People in learning organizations appreciate the connections they enjoy with others in the organization because they all have a united vision of the future. They help others learn by sharing ideas, suggestions and knowledge in open forums. They assume critical responsibility for considering where they can leverage their best possible contributions.

LEARNING WINDOW 6.1

"The single most important organizing principle of the late twentieth century and early twenty-first centuries is 'the wave.' The wave of change."

—*Dudley Lynch and Paul L. Kordis*

In a morass of conflicting ideas, the one constant that will keep the school on a focused course will be the quality of internal communication among schoolpeople. The more opportunities people have to communicate with one another, the more they will come to realize their capacity to learn from one another and have time to reflect on their learning. The construction of new knowledge in the learning organization is achievable only when people come together to share experiences, form intentions, and engage in a search for more information.

As people learn to adapt their roles in the system as a result of the acquisition of new information, they create new boundaries for themselves. Everyone gains in this optimized growth process. The best way to show the benefits of a quality improvement process is to allow workers to get involved in team sessions in which they are trusted with designing improvements in teaching and learning. People sell themselves on the merits of quality team learning by approaching every situation with high expectations, and they expand their capacities for growth by connecting with and testing the mental talents of their colleagues.

Human beings are born into the world with a need to cultivate relationships with other people. If they have allies and a support system within the walls of the school building, they can maximize their learning situations even in a world of high-speed transformation. When people operate in an organization that validates their contributions, they are encouraged to "let go," self-organize, self-direct, and reflect on how they can learn together to navigate the seas of change that exist in schools.

The education of schoolpeople about the promise of team learning is an enormous undertaking. To harvest results calls for looking at how schools can become learning organizations populated by a *community of learners*. This learning community has to be retrained on the merits of new team learning skills that specifically address: How to plan and manage and improve processes; how to work effectively in teams; how to establish reachable goals that don't overextend team members; how to coordinate support within the team; and how to interface with individuals who do not want to work with other team members.

It is always of utmost importance to remember that the best way to get others to change is for you yourself to change. After that, it is important to negotiate through the many forces that exist in the school culture that have a direct bearing on improvement of teaching and learning. The best way to influence change may be to ask questions about how the organization is currently functioning. Are there too many rules? Is cooperative planning part of the curriculum? Are some people mere cogs in the wheel when staff development topics are determined? Do employees in the school organization understand who the customers are? Who are the internal customers of the school? Why doesn't the school promote authentic assessment in all departments? Who is using cooperative learning most effectively in classroom instruction? How can teams improve the current situation?

One will be in a better position to construct answers to such questions by simply asking them aloud in team forums. Learning organizations allow individuals in the school to articulate concerns and, thereby, set the tone and purpose for team enterprises.

RESPONSIVE QUESTIONING

The concept of "responsive questioning" in team learning is one that I have originated based on my practical experiences in working with teams over nearly two decades of service as a school principal. Responsive questioning keeps the thinking process in constant forward motion in teams. Creative questions from colleagues cause all members to make inferences, create new mental models, and reflect on what is being said.

Responsive questioning occurs in team dialogue. Questions are posed and responded to in this dialogue forum. Action plans are developed based on the responses.

When we learn from others in teams we are constructing personal insights based upon the experiences shared by others. To obtain the very best understanding possible, we need to ask important clarifying ques-

---

LEARNING WINDOW 6.2
Responsive Questioning

✔ Inquire as to how the idea presented affects children or the school.
✔ Ask colleagues to introduce ideas about how to resolve the issue/project.
✔ Ask questions that trace issues which are peripheral to the topic. Analyze these sub-issues to see if they lead to "root causes." Ask clarifying questions.
✔ Call for new ideas to advance thinking on the topic.
✔ Develop a Plan of Action based on the responses.

tions about the ideas and events that are being related. When we choose to engage in responsive questioning, we create links between our world and the message that has been delivered from another place.

The social construct of teams is embedded in effective and lasting communication. We influence and, in turn, are influenced by one another in a continuous circle in the best teams. Team learning builds on the wisdom of all the players present.

People listen to and learn from questions. If they work in a school that offers a trusting environment, they will feel free to ask important questions and rally colleagues to pull together in a human network of thorough, productive reasoning to seek resolution to the object of concern. People feel validated and valued when they are part of a dynamic, action team that renders important decisions regarding school life.

How the groups elaborate their concerns and the content of their dialogue sessions will vary depending upon the task at hand. Initial questions in self-sustained, collaborative teams eventually translate into a final product. Teams pull together information, design activities, run projects, determine how to allocate resources, and make sense of disconnected— often disjointed—knowledge. A sort of social compact develops from the cooperation that develops in team endeavors.

The lesson of learning organizations is clear: Information is the new currency. Those schools that can adapt quickly to the ever changing environment will be successful. Therefore decision-making authority should be spread across the landscape of the school site to ensure quick responses and updates. The full participation of employees at all levels is necessary to capitalize on their insights in nonlinear, autonomous, tightly linked teams as they progress on their intimate, nonstop journey to expand learning parameters and open passages in the new learning organization culture.

THE CHALLENGE OF ATTRACTING SCHOOLS TO BECOME LEARNING ORGANIZATIONS

The quality movement has not been well received in our educational community. This is dismaying because it has been my great privilege to work with many outstanding teachers, support staffs, and parents over the years who want a quality educational experience for youngsters. They give a special meaning to schools in their daily interactions with one another and with students. Schoolpeople offer depth and sensitivity to issues that concern children. They are a source of human potential to create bonds of caring, compassion, and creativity in our schools.

Schools must learn how to engage these important people in risk taking, shared leadership, and high-performance teams instead of allowing them to be passive players who do not take responsibilities for even the most modest leadership roles. Learning organizations encourage people to take some control over their environment. They offer an opportunity for people who would otherwise be obscured in the maze of school bureaucracy to make collaborative decisions about improving the quality of school life.

Teams are a perfect fit for learning organizations because everyone in the system is involved in studying and proposing how to improve important processes. Learning organizations are connected systems that demand ongoing dialogue and informed interaction between workers about the processes involved in improving their work. When schools are left to the control of site administrators, uncertain objectives, parceling of information, and a general mystification about the vision of the school may result. Such cultures breed dependency. When teachers, paraprofessionals, parents, and community people are omitted from inclusion in decision making, widespread distrust about the mission of the school develops. In such a scenario, people are told what to think, not how to think.

Sometimes administrators, thinking that some schoolpeople are apathetic, assume that they do not want to be involved in teams. In other instances, the involvement of people is feared by principals because they think they will lose some degree of personal power. In either case, the result perpetuates an ineffective environment that insulates those directly engaged in work processes, sanctions only certain meetings and interactions, and limits the quality of teaching and learning. People will not diligently apply themselves to a task if they believe that there is no quality in what they are asked to do. Learning organization theory trusts in the intrinsic desires of people to do a good job. When people work in

---

LEARNING WINDOW 6.3

"Gold-collar workers, most of whom know their jobs better than their managers, will compose the majority of the workforce. Managers, as a result, will adapt to the new age by learning to use support people over which they will exert increasingly less control."

—Robert E. Kelley

a team, they work more ambitiously and accomplish more because they embrace the dual role of learner and developer.

The pursuit of learning should be a driving force for schools that want to join the ranks of other learning organizations. Schools, more than most organizations, should promote the message that we can no longer learn concepts and theories that will last a lifetime. Change is all about *us*. The contemporary view of people is that they are critical sources of emerging knowledge and unbridled creativity. Leaders of leaders emerge in such an environment.

Learning must be ongoing for all of us. We must each be engaged in learning how to learn. Learning and renewing are contagious. Momentum builds and gains depth when people are involved in a nurturing and sharing community that pursues self-improvement as a paramount strategy.

Leading management theorist Peter Drucker has said that the field of education will need to change more during the next three decades than it has since the modern school was created by the appearance of the printed book over 300 years ago.[2] Making the kind of meaningful changes that will be necessary will require that leadership in the school optimize the whole organization. Effective school practices cannot be piecemeal. There needs to be a new philosophy adopted within our school ranks for assuring quality education for all students and ensuring that all schoolpeople are included in the conversation about how to implement changes.

LEADING AT EYE LEVEL—NOT "I" LEVEL

Leaders of learning organizations have an inner geometry that multiplies emerging ideas. They draw strength from the significant contributions of team members—refining objectives, identifying details, and bringing depth and movement to the process. In our postindustrial society we have a plethora of ways to communicate, using available media, but nothing has the timeless power of an exceptional idea spoken from human to human. Ideas have an authentic energy of their own that is given shape and energy by leaders. Leaders in learning organizations create a social net that does not rely on working with unlimited financial resources. Instead, these leaders choose to rely largely on creativity, intelligence, and heart. They operate in flat, flexible structures, interacting, on even terms, with others in the organization at "eye level."

Leaders of learning organizations can rehabilitate schoolpeople who have lost their identity and feeling of worth by having been marginalized by the system. They can instill the necessary psychological and aesthetic rewards in schoolpeople so as to remove a brooding, yielding atmosphere and replace it with one that reconnects the human passion for achieving quality.

Leaders can bring an energy to the school that replaces the intractable silence with an open, loud, undefined yearning for transformational change. Leaders know that life is given greater purpose when individuals are allowed to congregate and share in articulate inquiry with colleagues about important issues affecting school life.

World-renowned marine biologist Jacques Cousteau once stated that, when you first enter the world of the ocean, you enter as part of the food chain, and you do not necessarily enter at the top. Similarly, leadership in the learning organization does not ensure a prominent role in all team dialogues. Leaders have no hierarchy to fall back on as a member of a team enterprise. Their value rests with the value and importance of the ideas they present.

Principals and other school leaders need to let team dialogue have a chance to "play out." They need to support slow engagement. People do not always participate in brisk and high-minded dialogue immediately after they walk through the door in team situations. You don't pick up a map at the entrance and move swiftly into great discourse about the issues that have befallen your school culture. Team dynamics are not that easy and take time.

It is to be expected that leaders will get lost in the ambiguities of team learning, everyone does. But leaders may welcome the experience. Ambiguity is sometimes desirable. As a team explores possibilities, ambivalence may serve the group better than absolute clarity. Conversations introduce the element of chance, and chance within the order of conversations is powerful. It is unexpected and continuous—always offering the possibility of innovation.

A treasure chest of ideas is presented in team learning that may be compared to courses at a dinner. The menu is deliciously adventurous. Everyone is invited to dine at the table and share his or her gift of insight and knowledge. It is always good to start leisurely and enjoy the flow of the conversation. One should now allow oneself to be shortchanged. Linger with the passages, embrace the nuances; take it all in. As the team leader, one should remember when to lead the dance and when to follow. Sometimes it is good to follow the path of the language embellishing rich ideas. Leaders do not have tenure in team dialogue. Leaders are not automatically at the top of the conversational food chain.

An architectural geometry unfolds as landscapes are defined and possibilities of the future become populated with inventive anticipation.

Dreams translate into mental constructions of mortar and stone in these sessions as people outline elaborate, cohesive structures for meaningful change. Every member of the team has talent to contribute to the cause. Some emerge as master artisans as they share their personal craft knowledge and, in so doing, guide the team to broader horizons of discovery. Reflective practitioners are born and prosper in team learning.

The conventional wisdom of learning organization leaders is to allow others to lead. The following passage, written over two thousand years ago is the best testimony I know about effective leaders in learning organizations.

> The cruel leader is he who the people despise;
> The good leader is he who the people revere;
> The great leader is he who the people say
> "We did it ourselves."
>
> —*Lao Tzu*

ADULT LEARNING IN THE LEARNING ORGANIZATION

For adults, the motivation required to achieve success in team or personal projects is based on a deep desire to achieve *competence*. On a psychological level, however, the driving force to achieve success is tied to a life-long need humans have to attain some degree of *independent* integrity in their world. And while the demonstration of competence gains the unwavering approval of team members, it is the longing for independence that replenishes one's desire to test new territory and take chances. Independence feeds our self-esteem. We feel good when we tackle challenges and emerge victorious.

Competence and independence do not evolve in separate worlds. They are not mutually exclusive in the course of human development. Both are important in the range of lyric human experience. The prompting issue for schools that express a desire to become learning organizations is how to create a structure that acknowledges competence while enabling self-esteem. How does one impart in the mind of the worker that the real organization you are working for is the organization called yourself?

There is no tried and true formula to support the emergence of competence and independence in a work setting for an individual. There are no privileged moments that will appear to help leaders guarantee implementation of a dependable process to ensure that all the needs of every person in the organization are fulfilled. The best leaders will recognize the importance of these human needs and attempt to establish an unpretentious framework that welcomes new and emerging ideas. The best leaders will establish processes that support the unspoiled beauty of easy access to ideas and information. An organization that operates as an open system— or, as Peter Senge says, a "seamless" system—will allow schoolpeople to tell their story.[3]

BEYOND PARALLEL PLAY

A concept exists in education known as "parallel play." It has to do with very young children in classroom situations who will go for hours, days, and even weeks sitting beside one another without acknowledging the existence of others. They are so self-engrossed with what they are doing that they do not interact with other children, even if it would be beneficial for them to function in a cooperative manner. Parallel play precludes any prospects for interacting or mutual learning.[4]

Unfortunately, many schoolpeople function in independent relationships, side by side, absorbed in their own work, performing in classic parallel-play sequences. They are unaware of the interests of others and see no value in joining forces with colleagues to solve issues such as improving teaching practices or enhancing learning situations for children. They build mental walls, then reinforce them with rigid behavior and stand in the corner of a classroom wondering aloud why the school is in the perplexing state it is in.

In the spring of 1996, I attended the Harvard International Principals' Center Conversation in South Florida. In one session, Dr. Roland Barth asked those principals in attendance to accompany him to the beach at Ft. Lauderdale to translate their vision of an ideal school for the twenty-first century into a sand sculpture.

LEARNING WINDOW 6.4
The Parallel Play

✔ Self engrossed.
✔ Nondynamic.
✔ Noninteractive.
✔ No opportunity for mutual learning.

It was interesting to note that the principals from China and Japan rolled up the pantlegs of their expensive suits, heartily waded into the ocean to retrieve sea water, and returned to the sand to build their prototype schools. The schools they created had beautiful gardens, picture windows, and innovative classroom arrangements employing the latest in technology. These schools were planned to be happy places—architecturally designed to promote interaction within the school, and open to the community at large, to welcome relationships from outside the edifice of the school.

Principals from urban areas of the United States, specifically Detroit and Chicago, built tall buildings that could not be easily accessed by either students or employees of the school. This arrangement precludes connecting with colleagues who may reside several full floors above! Most telling of all, urban U. S. principals constructed high, external fences, hoping to keep people *out* of their schools.[5]

It was especially insightful to see these very different final products, when everyone in the session was given the same directions and presented with the same mission. One group saw the advantage of having an open school, while the other chose to create a school that promoted parallel play. One group saw the possibilities of developing a rich support network with flat buildings connected to one another, while the other drew up plans for a school with tall structures reminiscent of a bureaucratic, top-down model that eschews collaboration in favor of self-interests.

It is time for the educational community to recognize the historical failure of parallel play for adults who work in schools. Years of unintentional isolationism in our profession have left us wounded and bleeding, behind closed doors, in tall buildings that cannot be accessed because we have locked other people out. We are now left to our own resources to survive. We cannot help one another unless we open our doors and attempt to communicate about the reality of where we are and our vision of where we want to be as educators. Furthermore, once this dialogue begins, we need to establish an unqualified OPEN HOUSE and invite support staff, parents, and community members inside our schools to help us transform them into true learning organizations.

Learning organizations promote "free play," not parallel play. They seek to open up the possibilities of timely conversations from all facets of school life about ways to improve schools. And although it may be true that the time frame for open dialogue has limits, the possibilities explored during the time that people are engaged shouldn't be. Open systems welcome the electricity of new and emerging ideas. They offer an opportunity to sit and reflect on the value of their content. Team members will tell you all you need to know. We need to listen to them, and we need to listen between the lines. The path toward improved practice comes from taking full advantage of evolving ideas developed within the ranks of school teams.

THE PACKET GAME

We can best maximize the talents of schoolpeople by ensuring that they have all the information they require to make important decisions regarding school life. Asking team members to build on other people's knowledge to improve teaching and learning practices, and to reflect on how to improve their own professional practice, is impossible if they cannot have access to pertinent information that may exist within the school organization.

One activity I have used with success with teams to promote the importance of sharing information to maximize the productivity of a team is the "Packet Game." I devised this activity because I truly believe that each individual in the school community has an intrinsic desire to make a contribution to the success of the school.

I have used the Packet Game with newly formed teams. As is the case in my school, the teams are composed of any number of teachers, support staff, parents, and the like. I begin by handing each of them a sealed 9½" × 12" envelope that contains information they will need to successfully complete a specified task. However, about *half* of the packets contain only two-thirds of the information that is required to successfully complete the task.

I ask the team members to sit independently and read the information, then to select a team facilitator and brainstorm together about how they will devise strategies to implement the project. It doesn't take long for the half of the team that does not have all the information to become aware that they have been provided with insufficient background knowledge to make effective suggestions on how to complete the project.

After awhile, I stop the proceedings and ask the individuals who have only two-thirds of the required information how they feel about their predicament. Some are angry. Others feel that they have been relegated to the status of inferior team members. Still others think the fact that they don't have all the information has to do with the premise that their opinions are not respected within the team.

All of these opinions are valid. If we fail to provide all the necessary information to the people in our organization to help us make effective decisions about school life, we are setting ourselves up for failure. To stimulate the talent available to us, we need to trust people to make the best decisions possible based on all the information that is available. People are our most important resource, and they will respond to the challenge of creating quality in our schools when we invite them into the circle and share what we know.

If we fail to share information in an open, timely, and equitable fashion about important issues, we jeopardize the entire team learning process. Team learning means we learn from others in an atmosphere that promotes open inquiry, advocacy, trust, and sharing. Teams that learn successfully share knowledge effectively. Team learning is about maximizing the talents of all team members.

FRAMING TEAM LEARNING

Schoolpeople participate in ongoing team learning by engaging in reflective dialogue, helping to construct an open organization, identifying new learning, understanding how to make application of this new learning, and implementing the words into action.

The Five Critical Elements to Framing Team Learning

1. **Reflective dialogue**—Communication that forms a basis for shared norms, beliefs, and values and launches plans for action. The ideas generated in reflective dialogue develop from the evaluation of ideas presented in team learning forums.

2. **Openness**—"Public," shared learning utilizing new methods to engage schoolpeople and implement changes in teaching and learning. Everyone learns in this environment—teachers, parents, administrators, support staff, and students.

3. **New learning**—Learning achieved after digesting and reflecting upon information generated in dialogue.

4. **Understanding**—Schoolpeople affirm common values and relationships supporting a collective learning process that is translated into action in teams.

5. **Modeling**—Team members internalize new learning and act based on reflective learning.

The five elements require people to get out of their self-imposed boxes, relinquish their egos, and embrace flexibility, divergent thinking, creativity, and change. Team learning is part of a uniquely human, reflective experience.

In Canada, Native Americans are referred to as the "First People." In contemporary education circles, educators need to embrace the role of becoming the "first people." Teachers and principals can advance the cause of powerful change by taking the risk to become leaders by creating an atmosphere for team involvement and open dialogue. The word "total" in Total Quality Management is significant. The school organization cannot be viewed as a collection of disparate pieces. It can be a single system with a common philosophy and purpose, led by people who collaborate in sustained personal involvement processes.

When we encourage others to share their story several things happen. Most importantly, an element of collegiality develops. This is an important factor in assisting potential team members past any initial awkwardness. It is also a paramount factor in developing a sense of evenness and trust in an organization where the breach of trust may have been the norm. Healthy dialogue propels people past stiff and rigid perspectives on key issues affecting school life and on to making connections. When team members open up and share their strengths, concerns, goals, and visions they, on a psychological level, surpass themselves. Team members can learn to trace their journey for change, to chart a personal map straight to the center of the self. When schoolpeople understand the power of the amalgamation of talent that exists within a team, they learn that it has a resonant, indefinable strength. They become uncommon people on common ground ready to reap uncommon profits from the experience.

When schoolpeople take the risk to open their collective classroom door to thoroughly explore the possibilities of advancing transformational change, they emerge from self-imposed exile in the school colony to extend their capacity to access and accumulate new knowledge and insights. The best way to evoke commitment from others is to be com-

---

LEARNING WINDOW 6.5

"The organization chart must be turned upside down. Middle management's role is to act largely as facilitator, greasing the skids and creating possibilities. Middle management is no longer to be the empire in charge of constraining, preventing or slowing down action in the name of turf. . . ."

—*Tom Peters*

mitted yourself. The best way to promote continuous learning is to be a role model for learning. A form of megacommunication develops when people interact in an open environment. On a cognitive level, people learn to maximize their learning. In such a culture, people are continuously enhancing their capacity to create what they desire to create. Authentic teams emerge when people come together with a sense of urgency to develop rich social relationships that lead to mutual trust which, in turn, causes individuals to embrace their personal responsibility to take on important leadership roles in the school.[6]

CHANGING STEPS

Change is difficult for everyone. It is easy for people to get into a groove, walking in "lockstep" uniformity with one's colleagues on a daily basis. Sometimes we don't even realize we are in such a rut. It is only when one recognizes an urgent need for change that one seriously begins to construct the shape it will take and to develop the capacity for altering course—to change steps, to change the cadence, and to walk down new paths.

In school teams, change occurs when the membership identifies the need to leave their comfort zone and move into the unknown. The vibrant dialogue that emanates from such an enterprise is an exciting adventure filled with lots of twists and turns. Sometimes teams run, sometimes they walk. The most dynamic teams are always moving ahead.

The meshing of team learning and individual search for self-knowledge is a perfect fit. Each pulls the other along to new experiences. It is important that the team go at its own "team pace." But just as the team moves along to uncover new ground, the individual finds special places to gauge

---

LEARNING WINDOW 6.6
Stem Questions about Maximizing Team Talent

✔ Why do some school administrators assume that school people are apathetic?
✔ How can leaders in schools sponsor meaningful dialogue opportunities for teams at school?
✔ Why is "parallel play" the norm for adults in schools?
✔ How does the "Packet Game" speak to the issue of inclusion for learning for all team members?

personal progress in learning about the primary project or peripheral areas of interest. Learning organizations allow for both. Team competence and individual independence are a recurring theme for a healthy learning organization. A reawakened, humanitarian heart beats in the best teams.

Teams in learning organizations discover their own pace. This is not to say that they do not have to meet deadlines. As a school principal, I understand how important deadlines are. What I want to suggest is that every effective team creates an internal pace and meter in their conversations. Sometimes this is a slow pace, which is perfectly all right. Sometimes it is good to slow down, pause, and reflect on learning. There are times when each person wants to experiment with ideas, pursue tangential thinking, engage in responsive questioning, or explore nonlinear possibilities. Deadlines can still be met, but it is of paramount importance for the team to accomplish schedules with a *quality product*. Quality is always the focus and guiding light for a learning organization. Quality comes about as a result of the thorough exploration of improving processes. Sometimes, in sifting through the multiplicity of ideas that emerge in dialogue, teams slow down to make certain they are choosing the correct path, the quality path. Slowness has its advantages. Learning organizations understand this and establish structures to invite all schoolpeople to participate in quality team learning experiences. Four such learning ventures are presented, in detail, in the next chapter.

ENDNOTES

1. Peter Senge, *The Fifth Discipline: The Art and Practice of the Learning Organization* (New York: Doubleday, 1990).
2. Peter Drucker, *The New Realities* (New York: Harper and Row, 1989).
3. Peter Senge, *The Fifth Discipline: The Art and Practice of the Learning Organization* (New York: Doubleday, 1990).
4. Roland Barth, "You Can't Lead Where You Won't Go," in Anne Turnbaugh Lockwood, *Research and Schools: Selected Investigations on Education Reform* (Albany, NY: State University of New York Press, 1997).
5. Gayle Moller and Marilyn Katzenbach, eds. *Every Teacher a Leader: Realizing the Potential of Teacher Leadership* (San Francisco: Jossey Bass, 1996).
6. Related by Larry Feldman, South Florida Principals' Center, at the Annual Principals' Center Representatives Council, Harvard University, October 22–24, 1996.

Learning Windows

6.1 Dudley Lynch and Paul L. Kordis, *The Strategy of the Dolphin: Scoring a Win in a Chaotic World* (New York: Fawcett Columbine, 1988).

6.3 Robert E. Kelley, *The Gold-Collar Worker: Harnessing the Brainpower of the New Workforce* (Reading, MA: Addison-Wesley Publishing, 1985).

6.5 Tom Peters, *Thriving on Chaos: Handbook for a Management Revolution.* (New York: Harper and Row, 1987).

CHAPTER

School Prototype Teams

"There is no success. There is only engagement. Any man who believes he has succeeded has settled for a limited engagement. At any time in one's life there is only the prospect of engaging more fully. If there is achievement, it is to be put by. Achievement is only what brings into view the next thing to be engaged."

—*John Ciardi*

"The test of first rate intelligence is the ability to hold two opposed ideas in the mind at the same time, and still retain the ability to function. One should, for example, be able to see that things are hopeless and yet be determined to make it otherwise."

—*F. Scott Fitzgerald,* The Crack-up

This chapter will explore empirical practice in team learning in the school culture. It puts the aspects of team psychology and communication to the test in team learning situations that I have experienced as a school principal. The four examples cited are inclusive of all players in the school community (students, parents, teachers, support staff, community leaders, and the school administration) in team enterprises.

They are easily replicated and, best of all, cost absolutely no money. This cost factor is extremely important for contemporary schools, which are often underfunded. It has always been a source of great personal dismay for me to read about schools that develop a prototype model of one sort or another to improve an aspect of learning, only to find that reproduction of the model is contingent on financial support from an outside sponsor. It is like being presented with a beautifully wrapped package that, under no circumstances, can be opened. Despite the allure of the way the prototype model has been carefully wrapped, it has a diminished usefulness for the intended recipient.

Schools that are the beneficiaries of such funding sponsorship achieve a comfort and confidence as long as the money supports the structure of their initiative. From my experience, these schools tend to make elaborate headlines for a while and are never heard from again. Once the funding source well dries up, the process dies. Even an unusually dynamic enterprise is almost never duplicated on a broad scale because the remaining 9 percent of schools do not have access to a large sum of money acquired from a grant, an endowment, or the government to implement the program.

Consequently, it is of extreme importance that the prototypes offered on the pages of this book be easily adapted to all schools in our society without any concern about funding. Quality is free: It is up to us to devise models that reach for it. All it takes is a team of committed people willing to apply their individual talents to improve student achievement. The prototypes in this chapter champion the possibilities of teams as a potent source of collective inquiry that promise to lead schoolpeople toward unparalleled self discovery.

The first team enterprise, "Extended Conversations," petitions teachers to interface with their colleagues in dialogue sessions to promote best teaching practices and produce innovative ideas about how to improve student achievement. The second venture, "Alternative Performance Assessment for Teachers," brings teachers and principals together to reduce the inherent isolationism of the teaching profession so they may learn to engage in sustained inquiry about how to improve teaching skills and create cutting-edge processes to upgrade learning in the classroom. The third presentation, "Principal Peer Assessment," is aimed at school leaders who desire to benefit from the existing craft knowledge of fellow principals. The final contribution, "The Instructional Transition Team," brings members of the entire school community—teachers, paraprofessional, classified staff, parents, business members, and school administrators—together to create a school action plan. The Instructional Transition Team (I.T.T) is not a School Site Council, Local School Leadership Council, P.T.A., or other formal entity of shared decision making, which have the purpose of lending advice to the school principal on sundry aspects of school life. The I.T.T. is a team of associates who use their collective resources and knowledge to create a unique plan for achieving goals aligned to the school vision.

These prototype teams conjure a shared opportunity for lasting communication about improving processes and practice. They give schoolpeople an opportunity to play a vital role as learners and developers of ideas to improve learning and teaching. As team members take part in these campaigns, they enhance their own capacity to create innovative solutions to the complex issues surrounding schools in our world.

EXTENDED CONVERSATIONS

The isolationism of teachers from other teachers is a prime factor in preventing meritorious teaching practices from being implemented in our schools. Benchmarking is nearly nonexistent in public schools because of this same seclusion. Schools that have quality teaching and learning practices in place could exist around the corner, yet no one knows about them because of a pervasive isolationism that exists in our school business.

As schools move into the next century, educators can design collaboration processes among themselves to share best practices. Quality management principles offer some hope for self-renewal in the professional development of teachers in team designs.

Initial Footprints

The initial footprints for the journey toward team learning were established at two of my previous schools, the Bandini Street School and the 153rd Street School, based upon the feelings teachers had about the need to connect with one another. The connections were internalized when teachers came to understand that they were all *internal customers* at the school site.

For example a fourth-grade teacher is the internal customer of a third-grade teacher because he or she inherits the students, and their accumulated knowledge, from the third-grade teacher the following school year. This practice is consistent with the teachings of Japanese quality management innovator Kaoru Ishikawa, who firmly concluded that the lifeblood of process flowed through the hearts and minds of individuals in an organization. Ishikawa defined the customer in an organization as "whoever gets the product next."[1] In the context of a school, the product to be passed along from teacher to teacher is the thinking ability of each child in the class.

The opportunities to talk about how to improve student achievement, digest the information as part of reflective practice, and then brainstorm specific applications doesn't exist in the school day. Of course, we have faculty meetings and staff development sessions, but these tend to be passive settings where teachers are being "talked to." My proposal was to have my teachers "talk with" one another and become actively involved in a team learning process as interacting, internal customers.

The Principal as Architect

I desired to create a format for teachers to learn from one another, as corespected practitioners. I wanted a school community replete with passionate, self-directed learners.

The importance of reaffirming our school vision of promoting a learning community in which every child would achieve success was a compelling force for all of us who realized the potential benefits of such a venture. It was because of the burning, collective vision of this corps of educators that a meaningful process was delicately carved. The sharing of new knowledge in internal customer teams was the format I envisioned.

It was Marcel Proust, in his classic *Remembrance of Things Past,* who wrote about the transformational shift of perceptions that occurs in people when we look at situations as beneficiaries of new knowledge. According to Proust, one did not have to actually pack up and set sail to distant places to gain a new vantage point. The real voyage is not in experiencing new landscapes, but in using new eyes.[2]

The opportunity zone at the school expanded as key leaders talked with others about the prospects of creating a conversational forum for teachers to talk about designing strategies to improve student achievement and share effective teaching practices. New eyes would clarify ideas and improved practices would be gleaned from the exchanges.

The Design

Released time was established at the end of designated school days to allow teachers to schedule "Extended Conversations" in internal customer learning teams at least twice per month. The central question that forged the underpinnings of the conversations: How to improve student achievement, our product at the school.

Teachers released their students to the playground for the final 35 minutes of the school day for physical education. My role was to supervise the children on the yard in assigned areas while the teachers converged in their internal customer teams in the library or a specific classroom to engage in their dialogue.

The internal customer teams were composed as follows:

TEAM ONE: Preschool and Kindergarten–First Grade Teachers

TEAM TWO: First Grade–Second Grade Teachers

TEAM THREE: Second Grade–Third Grade Teachers

TEAM FOUR: Third Grade–Fourth Grade Teachers

TEAM FIVE: Fourth Grade–Fifth Grade Teachers

TEAM SIX: Fifth Grade–Sixth Grade Teachers

An overarching theme to the undertaking was trust—my trust in them to be creatively productive and their trust in me not to interfere with them as they moved through waves of ambiguity. Placing teachers in an open-ended 35-minute conversation provided no assurance that productive dialogue would take place. On the other hand, if I imposed too many restrictions, or attempted to impose my own spin on how the proceedings should transpire, I might lessen their ownership in the venture and their possibilities to generate creative processes.

The real champions of change had to be the players on the teams. They would be the beneficiaries of personal and professional growth based on the connections they made and the energy they directed toward a collective purpose.

The Training Component

Initial training was devoted to a thorough understanding of the difference between dialogue and discussion. Dialogue is derived from the Greek word *Logos*, which translates into English as to be able "to reason with" in a free flow of shared ideas, whereas the more familiar word *discussion* denotes loudness and a clashing and banging of conflicting ideas. The emphasis in our teams would be on cultivating an honest and open dialogue that would center on how to improve teaching practices. The team members would be the source of stimulation and substance for the changes to be made.

Further training emphases included other desirable characteristics of effective dialogue meetings:

♦ Establishing ground rules.

♦ Attentive listening.

♦ "Supporting comments" and "responsive questioning" were emphasized as tools to enable individuals to gain better understanding and clarity.

♦ Cooperative rather than divisive dialogue.

- ◆ Ensuring that everyone has an opportunity to share out.
- ◆ Open and honest conversation focused on the topic and not on personalities.
- ◆ Optional areas included
    - ◆ Having a facilitator (many teams started out with one and after a period of time did not see the need).
    - ◆ Charting.
    - ◆ Keeping a journal.

As a framework for the dialogue opportunities, a few questions were suggested to the teachers for their initial meeting.

Initial Questions to Promote Dialogue:
- ◆ What do we want our students to know when they matriculate to middle school?
- ◆ How can we meet internal customer needs?
- ◆ What resources do we require to improve teaching and learning?
- ◆ How are we prepared to measure for success/quality?

Leadership that taps the human creativity of those individuals directly involved in a given process will always yield better results than leadership that imposes rules and authority. The freedom for teachers to explore the immense field of possibilities for designing new and innovative teaching practices in a risk-free environment animates the body and soul. All members of the educational community can arise from our self imposed "learned helplessness" to create practices designed to improve student achievement when afforded the opportunity to listen to other ideas about teaching and reflect on our own teaching practices.

LEARNING WINDOW 7.1
Schoolpeople

Old Paradigm	**New Paradigm**
✔ Isolated	✔ Collaborative
✔ Diminished role	✔ New leaders
✔ Limited access to information	✔ Involved in all decisions
✔ Cogs in the wheel	✔ Prime resource for the school

Measurable Outcomes

It is of interest to note that the dialogue that emanates from our internal customer format tends to carry over to recess and lunch breaks the next day, when teachers congregate socially. Hence the concept of an "Extended Conversation" ongoing and unbroken. The cycle of creative dialogue tends to move ahead, always characterized by a common thread of collaboration, never broken, just as continuous improvement reinforces the idea of always "leaning forward."

Some of the processes established during the school year, in the extended conversations, included:

♦ Establishing monthly outcomes by grade level and measuring them with "block tests" and teacher-constructed tests.

♦ Sharing authentic student work at monthly extended conversation sessions and establishing rubrics of quality work done by youngsters.

♦ Requiring science fair exhibits from each student enrolled in our school in the spring.

♦ Team teaching in reading and math to better meet individual student needs.

♦ Establishing the need for culminating portfolios from our sixth-grade students at the conclusion of the academic year, requiring them to demonstrate mastery in four domains:

　♦ **Self-Expression:** Express ideas in written form or by incorporating another communication media format.

　♦ **Academic Learning:** Be able to digest and reflect thoughts about written material from a text or library resource.

　♦ **Quantitative Reasoning:** Apply math knowledge to resolve real-life problems requiring analysis of contrasting information.

　♦ **Research Report:** Combine as many as possible of the above to produce an academic research paper or culminating project.

Summary

Our teachers took advantage of their opportunity to embrace conversation as a meaningful tool to develop meritorious visions of improving student achievement. As they presented their models of change to me, I marveled at both their ability to discover new truths about themselves and their intrinsic desire to improve teaching practices in this enterprise.

The dialogues have led to the establishment of standards and internal benchmarks that would, otherwise, never have been imagined. Teachers truly emerged as reflective practitioners on the path to become lifelong learners.

Furthermore, a collective bonding occurred. Once people became confident of their ability to manage processes, they sharpened their insights about the joy of learning. They understood that the concept of being a "lifelong learner" was not limited to their students, but also applied to each of them. By creating an infrastructure for internal customer conversations, a new tool was added to the professional educator arsenal. This learning tool helped our teachers clarify interrelationships, brainstorm possibilities, establish educational priorities, and plan/implement processes to improve the academic achievement of our youngsters.

The extended conversation format was designed to be successful for the participants. There were several training sessions with opportunities to practice in small groups, and an initial series of easily attainable projects was achieved so teams could gain confidence in themselves and their teammates. Teachers had no particular skills or experience with the process until they participated in training sessions. Training and the opportunity to practice in safe situations were the backbone of the venture. While the topics of conversation varied from one internal customer team to the next, the specific skills learned in training sessions kept the dialogue in familiar territory. Encouraging reflective conversations is a developmental process. There is much more for us to learn on this journey. We are only beginning to chart an expeditionary course toward self-discovery.[3]

Team conversations move people out of boxes. They offer dreams where an incarceration of the mind may have existed before. Once you hear the magic of provocative words of wisdom, new worlds open and old boundaries are forever altered. Extended conversations create new, eclectic worlds. They are a canvas for educators to experiment upon, creating no two paintings exactly alike. The authorship of the paintings ranges in styles from realist to impressionist to abstract, depending on the composition of the internal team skills and talents. They allow schoolpeople to go to places they don't usually travel. And to use new eyes in their journey.

AN ALTERNATIVE PERFORMANCE ASSESSMENT FOR TEACHERS

Performance evaluations are another exciting way to unleash the power of team enterprise. Two prospects for team involvement with assessment are presented in this chapter, the first of which deals with teacher evaluations.

Once again, the underlying theme of this process is to reduce teacher isolationism. If teachers are presented with the opportunity to give direction to the substance and content of their evaluations and have a mutual support system in place with their colleagues, they will view learning as a natural outgrowth of being a part of a learning organization.

A team approach to evaluation is a powerful means of promoting professionalism. I have used this process as the principal at three different schools and have always found that teachers will do more than is minimally expected because they tend to become immersed in the self-growth aspect of the venture. The level of interdependence and self-satisfaction garnered from alternative teacher assessment practices cannot be replicated through the old, standby, formal performance evaluation by the school principal. The standard, formal principal evaluation actually steers teachers into isolated, lonely, uninspiring, noncreative dead ends of despair. In the standard assessment process, teachers tend to try to meet the expectations of the principal, and in attempting to please the principal, fall into a trap. Teaching becomes a ritual and children become components of the daily ritual pattern of morning bell, reading, recess, math, lunch, social studies, physical education, and ending bell. Instead of engaging in rigorous and enriching academic processes that promote high expectations of children, teachers learn to play by the rules of the game, which deter risk taking and demean their role as an educator.

The alternative assessment process encourages the addition of options to the traditional evaluation procedures for teachers who have consistently demonstrated a high degree of competency. The goal of the alternative performance assessment is to encourage teachers to continue their professional development and personal growth. For teachers, the alternative assessment offers a critical window of reflective, powerful self-learning.

The premise of this engagement is based in the fact that professional educators can establish meaningful goals that will lead to increased professional interaction. Teachers should seek out the advice and assistance of

---

LEARNING WINDOW 7.2

"Most systems are designed to maintain themselves rather than change drastically. Mediocrity gets rewarded, which in traditional terms has been referred to as a 'regression to the mean.'"

—*Dudley Lynch and Paul L. Kordis*

colleagues in order to profit from their wisdom and strengths. Why is it always assumed that only the school principal is the all-knowing sage of teaching practice at the school? There is an abundance of talent lurking in the hallways and classrooms, in the form of highly qualified teachers who can share their talents in a nonthreatening venue.

Alternative assessment for teachers is a manifestation of dissatisfaction with the formal, principal evaluation procedure, which does nothing to promote professional growth and self-learning. This new assessment offers the possibility that teachers will enrich their learning by sharing creative and innovative approaches and focus on student achievement rather than on paying homage to the expectations of principals.

Goals

This assessment process encourages teachers to continue their professional development by recognizing that the most important interactions affecting student performance are those that occur between teachers and students. Increased student achievement can become a reality when those individuals making the most direct contact with students can collaborate in designing instructional strategies that will increase the probability of improving student learning outcomes.

As has been stated from the outset, a major goal of the alternative assessment process is to decrease the isolation of teachers from other teachers. The need for collegial dialogue about the art and practice of teaching to improve academic achievement is the centerpiece of this endeavor. The premise that informal, self-directed inquiry among professional educators will hold a greater "capacity to stimulate personal and professional growth in teachers" than will "elaborate, direct attempts," such as formal principal evaluations, is an important step in promoting a higher level of professionalism.[4] We are likely to profit most in a project when we are most committed to self-learning.

Description

Participants were permanent teachers with a minimum of four years of successful teaching experience in the Los Angeles Unified School District. The term "successful" was defined as having no "Needs to Improve" recommendations on the last two successive final district teacher performance evaluations.

Participation in the alternative performance assessment was strictly voluntary. It was the responsibility of each participant to agree to (1) establish meaningful goals that focused on professional growth and

(2) establish suitable criteria for the evaluation of the proposed growth to enter into the process.

The principal and teacher were required to reach mutually agreeable alternative evaluation options at a conference held in the beginning of the school year. At that time, two approximate dates for future conferences would be scheduled. The purpose of these conferences would be to encourage ongoing dialogue about the teacher's progress toward achieving the goals stipulated at the initial conference.

Evaluation Criteria and Options

The formal, district mandated, principal-teacher evaluations tend to do a disservice toward the goals of quality teaching. The needs of the teacher to engage in self-growth are not really addressed, and students' needs are addressed indirectly, almost like an afterthought or window dressing to legitimatize the process. The options in the alternative assessment process, listed below, were designed to meet the needs of all parties:

Portfolio
A teacher portfolio serves as a compilation of artifacts and materials selected by the teacher to document specific student learning that has occurred in the classroom. Sample inclusions may consist of a log of activities and lessons, samples of student work, examples of a newly developed curriculum, photographs, videotapes, or other forms of presenting student learning. Teachers are encouraged to seek out the help of colleagues to provide insights, information, and assistance with the development of a final portfolio.

Reflective Journal
The teacher may write in the journal about a specific learning strategy used with students during the year. The journal may serve as a mirror for a teacher's triumphs and disappointments in implementation of the learning strategy, citing specific examples of the experience. It is hoped that the act of written reflection about one's teaching can help each educator refine skills and increase self-confidence. The sharing of reflective journal entries is also encouraged in "Extended Conversation" team meetings as a starting point for encouraging dialogue on developing more effective instructional practices.

Peer Coaching
The intent of peer coaching is to provide feedback on a teacher's progress toward achieving specific areas of professional growth through a series of meetings that may include preobservation conferences,

classroom observations, and one-to-one dialogue sessions. The peer coach is selected by the teacher who is to be evaluated, based upon a perceived need to improve in a skill area in which the coach has expertise. The two teachers mutually agree to work, in incremental sessions, to ensure some degree of measurable competency in the designated skill area for the coachee during the course of the school year.

Classroom Action Research

The teacher (or a team of teachers) will select and identify a specific concept, instructional strategy, or theoretical approach, with relevance to classroom instruction, to be studied. The action research will involve an in-depth study of the effects of implementing a particular practice in the classroom. This research may be accomplished in conjunction with graduate course work. There is a plethora of possibilities within this option. Independent study of detailed research has direct implications for improving pupil achievement. The sharing of this research with colleagues may lead to a better understanding of the concept researched and promote further inquiry and research by colleagues.

Collaborative Study Teams

Participants meet for regular, information interactions by area of interest. The groups may choose to focus on a particular educational outcome area for student achievement or create a "study team" that does research or engages in an empirical practice that enriches the teaching staff. I have had study teams engage in researching numerous components of school life from early literacy to schoolwide discipline and sharing their findings with the faculty. One of the added features of this practice is that many teachers who serve on these collaborative teams are not doing so because they are being evaluated. They simply love the area of interest and serve on the team due to intrinsic motivation. Study teams are an excellent springboard for other team learning enterprises at the school.

Assessment of Outcomes

In planning meetings, the teacher and administrator determine future meeting dates to monitor progress. Prior to the end of the school year, the teacher and administrator meet to review the final accomplishments. A brief summary, which recounts the learning that took place, is placed in the teacher's permanent file at the conclusion of the year.

In the event that the alternative assessment process proves to be impractical, it may be discontinued by mutual consent of the teacher and administrator, and the evaluation will revert to the formal, standard procedure used by the school district.

The team building prospects offered in alternative performance assessments remove the cloud of anxiety associated with standard performance evaluations. Negative tension, which serves to debilitate and restrict, can change to creative tension that promotes collaboration and proficiency in this venture. Teachers in teams create an unlimited influence on the endeavors of others. Teams of teachers, working in harmonious accord, can fulfill the promise of raising the effectiveness of the entire teaching culture.

Teachers, in team enterprises, learn in new and enriching directions when they assume responsibility for their own evaluations, and share ideas and practice with colleagues in a process of examining and reflecting about what they do in the classroom. Teachers are leaders who lead other leaders in these enterprises.

Teachers can be advocates for improving their profession. They only need to concentrate their efforts to pull together in team ventures, holding themselves accountable for quality teaching while enhancing their capacity to create imaginative alternatives to the current, narrow, principal-directed performance evaluations that permeate the school community throughout the United States.

The liberalization of performance evaluations engenders some elements of risk taking on the part of the principal and the teacher. For example, the process may come under formal scrutiny from the superintendent or school board because it doesn't have a comfortable fit in the bureaucratic mind-set. The question to be posed is, "Do teachers and principals have a better understanding of the need to improve teaching practices?" Or do we continue to acquiesce to state legislatures, school boards, and superintendents, who devise these performance processes, to impose, from their vantage point in the sky, their perceptions of what effective teaching is all about. Remember, one tenet of TQM is to allow those individuals closest to the work to have a say about developing processes to better meet customer needs.

When teachers work cooperatively to promote change and improve teaching and learning in the school, great things are possible. The intrinsic desire of schoolpeople to address the human and intellectual needs of children will always lead us on the right path. Schoolpeople are ingenious individuals who desire to pass along the fruits of their wisdom to colleagues.

Teams that see the value of alternative evaluations celebrate the possibilities of self-directed learning. Many teachers, with years of experience with archaic and stoic performance evaluations, understand the damage that has been done by leaving teachers out of "the learning loop." Experienced teachers, my most important allies when introducing the alternative process, understand there is much lost ground that needs to be regained. Teaching is about lifelong learning and engagement with practitioners on the art and craft of teaching. Why have we in education insisted that it be pursued in absolute isolation?

Gary Latham and Kenneth Wexley, after ten years of research on performance evaluations, wrote *Increasing Productivity Through Performance Appraisal*. The following passage captures the history of top-down appraisals. They state that performance appraisals

> have little or no positive impact on (the evaluatee's) behavior. When criticism is included, performance frequently fails to improve and often drops to a level below where it was prior to the appraisal. Those areas . . . most criticized are least likely to show improvement.[5]

To change teaching, we must institute processes that give teachers a voice in their own learning. If the intent of performance evaluations is to improve practice, we need to stop the present process of betrayal and seriously engage in two-way communication about needs and expectations. The past does not have to be a prologue for the future. Those schoolpeople closest to the process have the strongest convictions about how important it is to take the necessary steps to change the current, rigid institutionalized practices. They can carry the message that a new order of things is possible in their penurious world. The national tragedy of teacher evaluations only exacerbates our national concern about the state of children's schooling. It is amazing that we do as well as we do when teachers have little control over many of their circumstances at work.

There is a general accord that teaching is an art. How can people be expected to create passionate, success stories about improving achievement with children in their classrooms when their opportunities for innovation and creativity are breached by an unsympathetic system which stresses conformity, rules, and dullness? Enlightenment and promise accelerate when schoolpeople have exciting practice to share with one another. It is profitable for everyone when there are many interesting people in the school community to talk with. A team approach to performance evaluations is a tool that enables the whole culture to stretch and test new waters.

Experience, tells us that, at least for some teachers, the traditional process of evaluation may not be the best model to promote professional growth. The alternative assessment process that I have used over the past four years is geared toward decreasing the isolation of teachers and improving collegial dialogue about the art and practice of teaching.

Participating teachers submit a form establishing meaningful goals and determine suitable criteria for measuring growth in achieving those goals. Options available to teachers include: teacher portfolios, reflective journals, peer coaching, and classroom action research. Alternative assessments encourage a critical window for self-learning so that teachers take an active role in their quest to become lifelong learners.

The Alternative Assessment planning form shown on the following page calls for the teacher and administrator to agree upon objectives and goals for the year and how they will be measured. The Alternative Assessment Summary calls for the teacher to reflect on his or her progress in reaching the goals. Ongoing dialogue between the teacher and administrator is the centerpiece of this venture. Professional growth is a collaborative enterprise.

PRINCIPAL PEER ASSESSMENT

Teams can be a valuable resource for a distinctive approach to personnel evaluations. The Principal Peer Assessment model was introduced as a liberating process to the top-down principal performance evaluation. My goal was to attempt to unclutter the tarnished, traditional process that was the norm for school principals in the Los Angeles Unified School District, by creating an intimate, personally satisfying process that would give voice to principals about their professional growth.

Principals deserve a condition to promote sharing the priceless, reflective knowledge they have acquired about their craft. An intelligent study of how to improve the principalship from within the ranks offers an optimization of the learning process for all concerned. The assessment procedure set forth in the following pages is a testimony to the continuing integrity and vision of my fellow colleagues who decided it was worth a try to take the risk to improve their professional learning. They realized, of course, that the greatest risk of all is *not* to risk.

Blueprints for a New Ark

Dr. William Ouchi, formerly of the U.C.L.A. Anderson School of Management, and Robert E. Wycoff, chairman of the LEARN (Los Angeles Educational Alliance to Restructure Now) initiative and president emeritus of ARCO, introduced the original concept of a New Skills Profile for school principals as the cochairpersons of a LEARN subcommittee in the spring of 1993. They produced a written skills profile that was, to the best of my knowledge, never seriously considered for any implementation by anyone in our school district. This excellent document sat nestled on a

ALTERNATIVE ASSESSMENT GOALS

Teacher's Name _____ Grade Level _____ Date _____

Teacher Prepares Prior to Conference with Administrator

Goals/Objectives (Will promote student achievement and/or instructional leadership.)

_____

_____

_____

_____

Quality Indicators (Criteria for how goals will be evaluated.)

_____

_____

_____

_____

Plans for Interaction with Peers* (Plan for at least two interactions.)

_____

_____

_____

_____

Approximate Dates of Administrator Conferences (2) to Be Held

Teacher's Signature _____

Administrator's Signature _____

*Peer coaching, classroom action research, collaborative groups only.

ALTERNATIVE ASSESSMENT SUMMARY

Teacher's Name _____   Grade Level _____   Date _____

Teacher Prepares Prior to Conference with Administrator

Goals/Objectives (Summarize the extent to which you accomplished your goals/objectives as written for the planning conference. Identify quality indicators used to measure success.)

_____

_____

_____

_____

Reflection on Teaching (State the extent that this process enhanced your professional growth. How did it affect student learning?)

_____

_____

_____

_____

Plans for Subsequent Growth

_____

_____

_____

_____

Review and Comments of Administrator

Teacher's Signature _____

Administrator's Signature _____

printed page in a LEARN manual—doomed to utter obscurity, until I chanced upon it.[6]

I was intrigued by the idea of employing many of these skills as learning tools, for an unprecedented peer assessment process for school principals. Properly inspired, I augmented the original profile items with some ideas of my own and conceived of a framework for implementation aligned to TQM practices. A team of principals was formed to establish parameters for activation—the main emphasis being for principals to construct some personal meaning for their professional development for the year.

Climbing Aboard the Ark

A revised New Skills Profile area of craft knowledge are charted below. This is an ever-evolving list which continues to be argumented as new skills are uncovered.

Principal New Skills Profile
♦ Knowledge of best teaching methods
♦ Leadership
♦ Budgetary competence
♦ Networking skills
♦ Technological literacy
♦ Team building
♦ Communication
♦ Application of best leadership practices
♦ Conflict resolution skills
♦ Diversity skills
♦ Systems thinking disciplines
♦ Total quality management principles

The initial cadre of volunteers willing to enhance their professional skills with the new assessment practice numbered eighteen. They were asked to identify from one to three skill areas that they desired to improve upon during the school year. They also selected master practitioners, who had expertise in selected skills areas, to work with during the year. These peers, working in teams of from two to as many as four principals, constituted a *learning family.*

From the beginning, it was understood that sincerity and trust would underscore a successful model. This venture was a definite voyage into uncharted territory. It would add a new and fuzzy dimension to the professional and personal associations colleagues had developed and maintained over prior years. It would take all the collective energy, mutual respect, and enthusiasm of the learning team for this newly designed enterprise to work. Indeed, in retrospect, it was the fervor for the project that was the impetus that kept the process constantly moving forward.

During the first year of implementation, a collegial personality emerged that sought out and valued connectedness and associations. The collegial alchemy that developed was the end product of an innate electricity born from working collaboratively. The opportunity to dialogue about how to improve practice, explore impasses, identify resources, and build shared meaning resulted in transformational change for the entire community of participants.

A View from the Ark

Preassessment conferences were held to establish growth expectations and to determine how support would be most effectively provided. Quality indicators were agreed upon to measure improvement. Some of the methods chosen for confirmation of successful realization of goals were:

♦ Establishment of a working portfolio

♦ Empirical observations

♦ Self-reflective journals

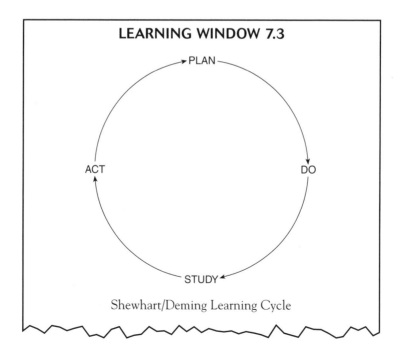

LEARNING WINDOW 7.3

PLAN

ACT

DO

STUDY

Shewhart/Deming Learning Cycle

- Peer coaching opportunities
- Written pre- and postassessments

By mutual agreement, a postassessment conference would be held at the conclusion of the academic year with master practitioners offering feedback on the progress achieved by the volunteer principals. A written essay, composed by the volunteer principal, would be filed subsequently with the region superintendent to comply with state mandates.

The Voyage

The complete process was aligned with the Shewhart-Deming PLAN-DO-STUDY-ACT cycle. This would be the framework for the peer assessment operation:

Plan
The initial "plan" phase for peer assessment was the direct result of principals expressing dissatisfaction with the existing evaluation process. Principals heard the rhetoric of reform, but didn't see results in my school district. In this instance, principals decided to stop moving in circles, and carved a path toward a new paradigm of self-discovery.

Do
Eighteen principals volunteered for the initial process. In this "do" phase they engaged in collegial sharing. Several principals thought this was the most valuable aspect of the operation. One noted, "I increased my resolve to reach my goals because of the absolute commitment I perceived on the part of my team members." Another principal stated, "The freedom to explore new dimensions of leadership was great. I found out that it was okay not to know everything, because the master practitioners I worked with told me they had areas that they wanted to improve upon also."

Study
This component of the cycle encouraged clarification of the goals and processes by the teams. To become reflective practitioners, principals had to have the opportunity to share their craft and access important feedback from colleagues. Team conversations offered the context for inquiry, sharing, and learning.[7] Principals bound together to merge into powerful learning teams because of the relationships nurtured during their sharing of craft practice. The volunteer principal's application of new knowledge was reinforced during these dialogue sessions. By openly conversing about problems and successes,

trust among all the participants slowly evolved. The transferring of the "concept to practice" approach was pioneered and cultivated extensively in these dialogue sessions, which took place on a regular scheduled basis designed by the participants.

Act
The "act" phase of this quality learning process took place in a final, year-end meeting to which all master practitioners and volunteers were invited. The act phase determines which format revisions or adoptions are to be made in the process for subsequent years. Recommendations were then recycled in the new framework for the next year. A year-end survey was passed out at this meeting, and dialogue ensued about the strengths and weaknesses of the procedures.

At this year-end meeting, there was general consensus that a weak point in the process was the lack of **time** for the participants to properly participate in face-to-face meetings. Another main point of contention was reflected in the recommendation that future volunteers limit themselves to attempting to improve in only one skill area during the year. It was agreed that it was unrealistic for quality improvement to occur for those individuals who had chosen two or three skill areas for the academic year. The most favorable response was that all eighteen principals wanted to do the process again, when their next district-mandated evaluation would transpire. Other commendatory remarks included: "I enjoyed being able to take control of the process." Another positive statement was: "The one-to-one relationship with a colleague enhanced my personal growth to a level I thought to be impossible." One fourteen-year veteran claimed, "I worked harder on this and got more out of it than any endeavor I ever participated in as a school principal." Still another declared, "It was great to go through the process . . . to develop quality indicators to validate ourselves as professionals. I am a better principal now than when I started because of this process." The bonding, in a safe and trusting environment, was an added plus that lent to the success of the peer assessment venture. It was a remarkable win-win experience for all concerned.

Transformation Change

By searching for personal mastery, participants clarified how to improve practice and broadened their visions of new possibilities of professional development. Organizations can learn only if individuals in them are engaged in profound learning opportunities. And the very soul of learning lives in the renaissance experience of self-discovery.[8]

The peer review process proves that intrinsic motivation is the most important aspect of transformational change in any organization. The pledge for self-learning linked all of us to a higher, intuitive desire to achieve some measure of professional growth. It was truly exciting to see how individuals gained new insights and assumed ownership of the process. The loftier link to another level of professional growth even caused disequilibrium within the principal culture outside our district. In the near future, we may see an expansion of the original concept to principals who are members of the Harvard University International Network of Principals' Centers. Dr. Joe Richardson, who coordinates many activities at the center at Harvard, has enthusiastically endorsed the concept of linking master practitioners across the nation in the future so that principals can benefit from the pool of talent that exists. Think of the possibilities of being able to access banks of collegial expertise by using e-mail, or on the Internet. In time, all of this and much more will come to pass.[9]

Quality

Since the premise of the framework for the assessment process is based on total quality principles, it is important to make a comment about the quality of the venture.

Principals have been invited to recommit their considerable skills and energies to a process that has personal meaning for them. They have chosen to set sail on a missionary voyage to "reframe" the context of their learning. To do so, they relinquished the relative safety of the tried-and-true traditions of a biannual district evaluation mechanism that was unproductive, static, and stale. Most school districts have similar processes in place and are stymied with the same inertia. What is needed to change this predicament is a new approach.

By understanding that we, as a group of principals, were the ones who would define the quality of our experience, we moved to personal levels of accomplishment heretofore not fathomed. It was not only arriving at our destination which was important, it was the voyage that was most gratifying. Team learning proved to be a vehicle for growth and profound self-reflection. Our field of vision of the possible became a "calling" for a crystal-clear field of dreams.[10]

There is a classic superstition, passed along through the ages by sailors, that—in time—one enormous wave, known as the Ninth Wave, will plunge across the seas. It is the most powerful force known to mankind. The ultimate goal of each mariner is to catch the Ninth Wave at its crest, to harness its expansive power, and ride it safely to shore. This requires great skill, ingenuity, daring, and risk taking.

Such a wave exists in the future of education, and specifically for school leaders. To catch the Ninth Wave, we must reaffirm our desire to become high-level risk takers and be prepared so that, when the wave approaches its peak, we may be able to catch it and ride it all the way to shore—to our destiny.

The Principal Peer Assessment model moves us, as an educational culture of lifelong learners, closer to catching the elusive Ninth Wave. It is both hazardous and exciting at the same time. The seas of change are chaotic and treacherous. However, our vision for self-growth may be so profound that we are compelled to rigorously proceed forward into uncharted waters. The Principal Peer Assessment enterprise may cause some leaders in other school districts to hoist up the sails of their ship of discovery in a sea of change.

The Ninth Wave is fast approaching.

QUALITY IMPROVEMENT PROCESS
PRINCIPAL PEER EVALUATION

Plan for Quality	
	1. **Identify output** *Desired state: Peer evaluation*
	2. **Identify primary customer** *School principal*
	3. **Identify customer requirements** *Select from new skills profile*
	4. **Identify supplier specifications** *Align with TQM principals, transfer into own language requirements: Initial Plan Sheet*
Organize for Quality	
	5. **Identify steps in work process** *Ownership, planning, selection of skill areas and members, benchmarking talent, and establishing deadlines*
	6. **Select measurements** *Quality indicators and quantitative/qualitative methods of measurement*
	7. **Determine process capability** *Periodic meetings, GAP analysis, constant communication*
Monitor Quality	
	8. **Evaluate results** *Measure against Initial Plan Sheet template with Final Peer Assessment and Self-Assessment*
	9. **Recycle** *Profound knowledge, consistency of purpose, continuous improvement, refine process for next year*

FORM 1

PEER ASSESSMENT INITIAL PLAN FORM

After completion, this form is to be attached to the Initial Plan Sheet and given to the cluster leader.

Name _____ School _____

Peer evaluator _____ School _____

New Principal Skill Profile area of focus:

_____

Proposed strategy, plan, project to improve competence:

_____

_____

_____

_____

_____

_____

How will improvement be measured? (Quality indicators)

_____

_____

_____

_____

Completed by _____   Date _____

Evaluatee _____   Date _____

Master practitioner _____   Date _____

Cluster leader, evaluatee, master practitioner (one copy each)

FORM 2

FINAL PEER ASSESSMENT FORM

The peer evaluator will complete this form. The final peer assessment review will be discussed with the evaluatee, initialed and given to the cluster leader.

Name _____   School _____

Peer evaluator _____   School _____

New Principal Skill Profile area of focus:

_____

The evaluatee

- ❏ Satisfactorily made progress to improve competence in the stated area of focus in his/her Initial Plan Form.
- ❏ Did not satisfactorily make process to improve competence in the stated area of focus in his/her Initial Plan Form.

Method(s) used to measure improvement:

_____

_____

_____

_____

_____

_____

_____

Evaluator (Initial) _____   Date _____

Evaluator (Initial) _____   Date _____

Cluster leader, evaluatee, master practitioner (one copy each)

FORM 3

SELF-ASSESSMENT FORM

Name _____ School _____ Date _____

Self-evaluation:

_____

_____

_____

_____

_____

_____

_____

_____

_____

_____

_____

_____

_____

_____

_____

_____

_____

_____

_____

_____

_____

_____

Cluster leader, evaluatee, master practitioner (one copy each)

THE INSTRUCTIONAL TRANSITION TEAM (I.T.T.)

The final prototype team learning model to be presented in this chapter is the Instructional Transition Team. This team is composed of all segments of the school community: teachers, classified workers, paraprofessionals, administrators, parents, and community workers. Their consuming work: to create an action plan for the school to improve student achievement.

Creation of a distinctive plan that presents a clear picture of the school and where it is heading is a difficult task. This was a reality check of the greatest magnitude when our team first met. We found that we did not have a unifying, schoolwide vision and had disparate ideas about where we, as a school culture, were traveling. To further cloud the situation, many of the members of the team had no experience writing a school plan. We were fledgling angels, trying out our wings for the very first time.

Add to the mix a group of savvy teachers and classified staff members who had experienced the sordid reality of working with the school system bureaucracy and its customer unfriendly appendages. They knew that to present any plan that would be too innovative or fresh or controversial would only provoke the sacred bureaucracy. For these people, I became painfully aware of how very difficult it is for those who have always known poverty to better themselves.

All members of the school community were invited into this swirl of anticipation. The composition of an instructional transition team may vary, but a good model would be: four parents, one or two classified staff, one paraprofessional, four teachers, two community people (preferably from the business community), and one school administrator. The size and composition can be customized to meet the needs of the school. The most important aspect of the enterprise is to get a combination of new and seasoned people who are capable of great insight together to crisply articulate their point of view on how to improve the school. The best I.T.T.s have people who are optimistic about children, have creativity in their blood, want to focus on improving student achievement, can work within a team framework for an extended period of time, have a plethora of ideas to share and, most importantly, are good, active listeners.

Conversations about how to improve teaching and learning, which will lead to a written plan, have to take many factors into consideration. It is important to balance all sides of issues before creating a plan on how to improve learning processes. People who listen carefully discover insights that can lead to purposeful inquiry about how a school can build a better capacity to improve itself. There are no shortcuts in this journey. Everyone is a leader and everyone is a learner.

To further emphasize this point, I am reminded of the ancient Chinese saying:

> Be not afraid of growing slowly,
> Be only afraid of standing still.

The Work to Be Done

The I.T.T. is fully committed to probing the possibilities of long-term change processes to better the school. Each team is unique because the group interactions within the team lead them to develop models for change that are indigenous to that school.

The I.T.T. asks all shareholders to examine schoolwide beliefs and how they affect teaching and learning. Once the I.T.T. gets a clear, comprehensive picture of qualitative and quantitative information, as presented in student work, classroom practices, and test scores the team is able to identify strengths and weaknesses. From this background, they develop an action plan designed to support improved learning and teaching practices.

The I.T.T. asks, "How can we do better?" What specific outcomes do we wish for our students? Who needs to be involved in the planning and implementation stages? What individual responsibilities need to be assigned? How do we work more effectively together?

The broad base of this team ensures that the voices of all shareholders are included in developing an effective plan of action. I.T.T. members represent a multiplicity of perspectives. They are committed to leading long-term change, and they assume a supportive role for other team members, encouraging them to participate and share leadership roles.

LEARNING WINDOW 7.4
I.T.T. Key Actions

✔ Have a clear purpose.
✔ Ask for input from others in an open forum.
✔ Generate ideas.
✔ Evaluate ideas.
✔ Establish team goals.
✔ Identify individuals who will champion the goals.
✔ Establish subteams (if needed).
✔ Establish time lines.

In my experience with I.T.T.s, there must be regular and frequent meetings that encourage sharing ideas, asking questions, and reflective conversation. A process for continuity in planning, analyzing, and ongoing self-learning is important.

A clear agenda should be in place for each meeting, and an I.T.T. leader (preferably not the principal) should be identified by consensus. Meetings should challenge each team member to examine beliefs regarding what the school should "look like." When people come to a consensus about a school vision, they are better able to design plans to change structures to support and better facilitate high levels of student performance.

The creation of a School Action Plan is the final product of the I.T.T. There are many aspects of school life that affect student achievement. The following action plan items are meant to serve as a guide for study and may be desirable to include in a customized plan for your school.

- ◆ **Governance**
  Describe how collaborative decisions are made at the school. Consider membership, roles, and responsibilities, and decision-making processes to be implemented.

- ◆ **Expenditure Plan**
  Include a school budget that specifies categories of money received and how it is to be spent.

- ◆ **Parent/Community Involvement Plan**
  Define how parents and community members are to be involved in student improvement activities.

- ◆ **Training**
  How will the professional development of all staff members bring about changes that will result in improved student achievement?

- ◆ **Accountability**
  How will accountability for continuous improvement at the school be determined? Measurable student achievement outcomes should be linked to specific processes and specific teaching and learning strategies, preferably aligned to authentic assessment.

- ◆ **Measurement**
  How will the school's progress toward achieving school plan goals be measured?

- ◆ **Waivers**
  What district policies stand in the way for improved teaching and learning practices to take place?

The school action plan is a school growth plan. The I.T.T. engages in deliberate, purposeful inquiry to design processes to be used to solve problems and implement processes critical to creating meaningful change in teaching practices that will directly lead to improved learning. The bond that holds the I.T.T. together is the united passion to create the best school possible: a quality school.

New Directions

The I.T.T. is an enabling forum that encourages participants to challenge past assumptions about how schools work. The team works interdependently—parents, community, paraprofessionals, teachers, classified staff, and administration—to advance their collective vision of a quality school by sharing information in open dialogue, identifying resources to achieve project goals and align systems, policies, and processes. The broader the spectrum of representatives on the I.T.T., the more diverse the perspectives and the better the final product.

Periodic I.T.T. meetings lead to rich sources of learning. They are an excellent example of an adaptive, response team that values and validates the contributions of all people. School organizations that herald the importance of bringing a broad base of talent to the table to dialogue about how to improve teaching and learning practices will have a better chance of meeting future needs than those who fail to recognize the talent that exists in their school community.

The possibilities of progress for schools are as many as the directions on the compass. The prototypes offered in this chapter may encourage fur-

---

LEARNING WINDOW 7.5
Stem Questions to Reflect on the Empirical Examples
of Team Learning Presented in This Charter

✔ What applications from these true-life examples do you envision at your school?
✔ What barriers exist to prevent them from being replicated?
✔ How can you work within your organization to overcome these barriers?
✔ What new learning have you experienced at your school that you would like to share? How can the practices shown in this chapter be implemented to help you?

ther investigation of possibilities for profound change. When men and women are given the opportunity to connect about important issues affecting schoolchildren, they contribute to a greater fulfillment of human potential. The ideas they generate can become new directions of thought to lead to improved student achievement.

All of the team processes presented in this chapter emphasize that it is not where schoolpeople are at a given place and time that is of paramount importance, but rather *where* schoolpeople are going that matters.

ENDNOTES

1. Kaoru Ishikawa, *What Is Total Quality Control? The Japanese Way*, translated by David J. Lu (Englewood Cliffs, NJ: Prentice-Hall, 1985).
2. Marcel Proust, *Remembrance of Things Past* (New York: Random House, 1986).
3. James E. Abbott, "Extended Conversations," *The Total Quality Review*, November/December 1995.
4. Roland Barth, *Run School Run* (Cambridge, MA: Harvard University Press, 1980).
5. Gary Latham and Kenneth Wexley, *Increasing Productivity Through Performance Appraisal* (Reading, MA: Addison-Wesley, 1981).
6. James E. Abbott, *The Restructuring of the Los Angeles Unified School District: When Dinosaurs Learned How to Dance* (Las Vegas: Q.M. Press, 1994).
7. Debra L. Morehouse, *Total Quality Management* (Shawnee Mission, KS: National Press Publication, 1992).
8. James E. Abbott, "The Renaissance Principal: Leading the Movement to Transform Education," *The Executive Educator*, September 1994.
9. James E. Abbott, "Measuring Quality with Fuzzy Logic," *The TQM Magazine* 8, No. 4 (September 1996).
10. James E. Abbott, "Sharing Craft Knowledge: The Soul of Principal Peer Assessment," *Technological Horizons in Education Journal*, November 1996.

LEARNING WINDOW

7.2 Dudley Lynch and Paul L. Kordis, *The Strategy of the Dolphin: Scoring a Win in a Chaotic World* (New York: Fawcett Columbine, 1988).

CHAPTER

A Life of Significant Contention

"There is a time for departure even when there's no certain place to go."

—*Tennessee Williams,* Camino Real *(1953)*

I remember covering a fifth-grade classroom for a teacher one afternoon a few years ago. The topic of inquiry was Dr. Martin Luther King. I posed a question to the class about whether they thought Dr. King was a "student." One child raised her hand and responded, "He was a student because he graduated from high school"— an interesting answer. This school was situated in a very poor neighborhood, and the child's frame of reference for becoming educated was limited to getting a high school diploma. She didn't think about how Dr. King or others could continue their learning by going to college, or continue their learning from life experiences beyond high school. Her perception of a student was limited to her personal mental model.

It is part of our Western culture to frame our understanding of learning in terms of attainment. We "get" a high school diploma. We "graduate" from college. We "get" a job. Does learning continue after one achieves these goals? Can we learn from life and work experiences when we share knowledge? Dr. King significantly changed our society by choosing to contend with the complex issues of his day. He met the challenges of his times head on, electing to live a life of significant contention, learning along the way in his life's journey.

Quality organizations encourage continued learning. Team learning promotes lifelong learning. The unapologetic premise of this book concerns exploring the possibilities of continuing learning for schoolpeople

---

LEARNING WINDOW 8.1

"The paradox of rising expectations helps us better understand why it is on the best campuses that there is the most restlessness and demand for change."

—*Richard Farson*

---

in team learning situations at work. School leaders should be role models for leading a life of significant contention to improve our schools.

How do we encourage people to feel an urgency for change? How do we motivate individuals to move beyond following the routine of the day, and to choose to break through to assume ownership of it? How can team learning be fostered in our schools?

We can get people involved so that they meet the challenges facing schools by promoting their ability to work collectively together in meaningful work enterprises. There are no absolute answers for each case, however, the introduction of team learning in the school culture may be a beginning. Teams can open doors for people who have felt disenfranchised by validating their contributions on projects that are deemed important by colleagues and the school administration.

The validation of contributions by schoolpeople improves morale and encourages more ideas about how to improve other processes. When individuals feel they are not appreciated or are unable to influence the direction of their work, their morale and productivity decline.[1] They wind up traversing a life of narrow passages—much like school hallways, limited and with sharp corners. Teams reassert that we are in a people profession. Everyone at school should be considered a professional resource for the improvement of teaching and learning. Everyone can learn from the contributions of other team members.

ORGANIZATIONS GROW ONE CONVERSATION AT A TIME

The crisp language of team learning is an unfailingly admirable venture. Ideas expressed in teams strive to break down old boundaries. Team dialogue offers a kind of sanctuary for imaginative thought that is essential for self-recovery, reconciliation, and reinvention.

Transformation of our schools cannot happen with top-down edicts from educrats, or the fractured syntax of schoolpeople whispering in hallways about all that is wrong with a school or school district. It must occur in school organizations that have leadership promoting imaginative projects by schoolpeople. These schools must have leaders who desire to walk the talk of significantly contending with the difficult issues of school life. They lead a life of significant contention.

Team learning offers all the promise of involving the formidable intellect of the human resources of the school to construct meaningful solutions to pressing issues. When ideas are presented in open spaces, they acquire a reality and foreshadow the slow extinguishment of the bureaucratic order. New learning evolves in discrete stages in such an atmosphere.

Team learning offers a sort of poetic introspection for people. It flows not in some intricate alignment, centered by the force of gravity, but more asymmetrically, governed by people who learn to ask the right questions about how to improve teaching and learning.[2] The conversations flow in the direction of the value of the ideas which are presented in the exchange. The promise of team learning is that, when schoolpeople come together to work in teams, they not only participate in their own learning through discovery and self-reflection, but they also learn to draw upon others on the team to gain new insights.

COMMUNICATE FOR UNDERSTANDING

When team members connect with others, they build a sense of community. This union helps to create and sustain conditions that allow everyone in the school to learn. Ideas tend to spark ideas from others. It is a fact of life that personal breakthroughs result more often from chance opportunities than from conscious design. This is one of the great attributes of slow, self-paced, reflective dialogue in teams. Peter Senge believes firmly that learning is "rooted in conversations."[3] When listeners are alert and concentrating on the simplicity of the words that are spoken, their vision of conceivable application of the words achieves a focus.

The whole notion of chance is in the air with every conversation. The orthodoxy of chance can be traced to Mozart, who experimented with making music by throwing dice. Later, French visual artist Marcel Duchamp created a whole aesthetic around chance occurrences in art. Chance in conversations negotiates a fine balance between the literal and metaphoric, the timely and the timeless. What might appear to be disparate words spoken in team dialogue sessions, can, through juxtapositions, unleash unanticipated ideas in the minds of colleagues. These ideas are then formulated into spoken words that, in turn, spark urgency in others. Sometimes the words provide an ethereal message in listeners, inspiring them to cast aside the mundane, in search of the extraordinary.

Chance permeates the arts. More than any painter of his generation, Manet devised a way of seeing—a new form of optics—for his artistic epoch. Leadership is also an art. Leaders, who understand the value of team dialogue, encourage schoolpeople to craft artistic paths which will enhance professional and student learning. The subtle messages of conversations, like a late-afternoon light filtered through trees, permeates the psyche. As people learn to decode the words, they employ new learning to formulate a course of action for achieving team goals.

Talented, self-directed schoolpeople change their organizations one conversation at a time. Team learning is about efficacy of individuals. When they are provided with a forum for dialogue they learn to deliver a clear message for quality in schools from their hearts and minds.

Organizations grow as individuals realize their capacity to make positive contributions to the culture. The interpersonal relationships made in networking situations support and validate successes of others. When information is freely shared, people assume a "we" attitude in a seamless organization. This "we" attitude is a bold, ambitious feeling among people that translates into optimistic language in team dialogue. Team learning offers participatory, sustained, ethical engagement about significant contention. Team learning offers individuals an opportunity to reach out from the inside to touch the light and feel the heat.

A life of significant contention by schoolpeople is required for transformational change to take place in schools. It is important for schoolpeople to be in a constant dialogue leading to self-discovery. School leaders desiring to construct a framework for self-renewal, collaboration, participatory decision making, new leadership roles, open inquiry systems, and quality approaches to teaching and learning will embrace the possibilities of team learning.

When schoolpeople participate in team learning enterprises, and have their ideas and initiatives recognized as legitimate strategies, they will apply themselves even more vigorously at work. In his landmark research, Douglas McGregor saw that, when people were invited to participate in meaningful decisions regarding their work, their productivity increased proportionately.[4] There are many schools in our society that belong to school districts. Quality schools belong to the teachers, support staffs, parents, and students too.

OPEN MESSAGES

Attempts to circumvent the layers of school bureaucracy can be risky business. One will accept the risk only if one assumes he or she has a stake in the game. When we accept a life of significant contention, we assume we can truly change the fabric of the school culture.

It is only through living—the experiencing of life—that individuals find new levels of personal development. Worthwhile goals are worthy of risk taking. People who desire change need to consciously seek out others who feel the same way. Their conversations may lead to dialogues with other people who feel similarly committed to change. One means to connect rests with school teams engaged in team learning. Teams can serve to satisfy the hunger for contentious change.

There are multiple avenues for initiating important change at schools. Teams are but a part of a larger, integrated, evolutionary process. Nonetheless, they are a vital aspect of achieving lasting results. People who pull together with a common objective can make a statement about how they do their jobs, how they are to be assessed, and what a rich resource they can be. In their collective wisdom, they can help shape the reinvented school organization.

The best teams have a united sense of urgency about their objectives, which will serve to ruffle the complacent and inspire the visionaries. By communicating their progress, successes, and new knowledge with everyone, teams affect the entire social and work fabric. This may inspire recruitment of others in the school community to leave their self-imposed comfort zones as they sense an urgency for collaborative change.

LEARNING WINDOW 8.2
A Plan of Action

✔ What activities would you enjoy seeing more frequently at your school? Less frequently?
✔ How can dialogue improve professional commitment at your school?
✔ What can you initiate tomorrow to change an aspect of school life?
✔ How can you begin a life of significant contention? If you cannot change, then who?

Teams gain understanding and commitment from others in the school when they establish a process to welcome and encourage total participation. This participation may exist in formal team structures that have specific goals to achieve, or they may occur in informal, ad hoc teams, that work as study teams seeking to resolve issues affecting broader school life.

The best teams get schoolpeople to ask questions about variables in school efficacy with regard to instruction, teaching practices, decision making, goals, vision, outcomes, and use of resources. From initial stages, collaboration and continuous reconceptualization can become a very real part of the school. It comes down to open communication in an open system. When people communicate constructively, show mutual respect, and have a common belief system, change will occur. In *Diffusion of Innovations*, Everett A. Rogers reveals that, when a mere 5 percent of a culture accepts a new idea, it becomes firmly imbedded in the belief system of the population. He goes on to state that when 20 percent are in accord with the idea, it's unstoppable.[5]

Open systems address the issue of how to get people to work together toward a common objective. Self-confident, cohesive teams attract new members who generate new knowledge and innovative approaches to improve school life. They challenge erroneous beliefs and long-standing teaching practices as part of a fluid inquiry process that features an inclusive commitment to accountability, shared understanding, and a desire to make classroom teaching and learning more engaging.

DOING BUSINESS IN A GLASS HOUSE

Leadership in schools is being recreated. The movement toward quality in schools must begin with developmental processes such as the school principal's providing support and encouragement for schoolpeople to share promising practices, craft knowledge, and other experiences in team situations. These opportunities may influence teachers to leave the safety

---

LEARNING WINDOW 8.3

"We must make the necessary shift in our mind set so that our thinking is aligned with the new realities of the world of work."

—*Price Pritchett and Ron Pound*

of their classrooms to join with classified staff members and parents to become advocates for improving instruction at the school.

Teams add a new dimension to relationships among all schoolpeople. As people learn to share actions, insights, and information, they create newfound knowledge about how students learn, how to improve teaching techniques, and how they can assume more responsibility for changes in curriculum areas, pedagogy, and even the structure of the school.[6]

The participation of principals is critical in supporting schoolpeople who choose a life of significant contention. Quality schools depend on quality adult interactions. The days of fractured relationships among teachers, support staff, and parents are slowly becoming a fading image in the rearview mirror of the school traveling on the fast track toward quality. A viable school community that values the input and inquiry of schoolpeople in an open market is the preferred school organization for the new millennium.

Input is required to keep the school culture fresh with new ideas. Inquiry must be part of a never-ending process, just as learning is a never-ending process. Inquiry is a process that may serve to unify "professionals and lay people."[7] When people acknowledge that something is not working effectively, they can proceed to change it without blaming anyone in the school family.

Contemporary school administrators work in glass houses. Model leaders embrace collaborative approaches to assist professional educators to enhance their practices. Required curricular changes, assessment criteria, classroom configurations, improved student outcomes, and reflection opportunities demand involvement of many people from diverse backgrounds. The prospect of school team learning offers one of the best hopes we have to create fundamental changes in schools today.

The best school leaders will act as servant leaders, situating themselves so as to provide stewardship for people coming together to interact about needed changes in the school organization. They know that there are many leaders in every school and that they need to fulfill the role of encouraging schoolpeople to participate in developing policies and processes that will improve teaching and learning.

When school leaders do business in a glass house, they generate a process for self-renewal. School leaders must seek out the most creative people in their culture to design the kind of visionary change in order to precipitate lasting change. Schoolpeople have been left out of the "conversational loop" far too long. We've seen the empty results of myopic, top-down leadership in our schools. The opportunity to pursue implementation of total quality management practices is within the grasp of the school leader who looks to the horizon, and not to the bottom line.

MIND MAPPING

Credendo Vides means not "seeing is believing," but "believing is seeing." Leaders in schools can direct the importance of creative visualization. When one relies on the human spirit, anything is possible. If schoolpeople engage in elaborate dialogue about what schools can become, and if we truly let our minds go, we can gaze upon scalloped clouds in the sky and construct quality-led school castles in their place. These are lofty expectations for schoolpeople who, in some instances, may feel that they have been under house arrest.

However, school leaders can insist on involving everyone in fostering a new agenda, challenging old assumptions and icons, and repositioning people's thinking about what schools can become. They can sponsor a prevailing belief that each member of the school community is capable of adding to the overall knowledge bank of the school culture and of learning from every other member.

In such schools, a state of mind develops which values the intellectual capital which exist among schoolpeople. Schools can become "Knowledge-Creating Schools." As schoolpeople invent new knowledge, they address the personal issue of reinventing themselves. All new knowledge originates with an individual. When that individual has an opportunity to share his or her insights in an organization that promotes team learning, he or she helps others overcome preconceived limitations.

There is a precept in schools—that has existed for far too long—of "privileged knowledge." A code has been imbedded in the school world: Teachers should teach and students should learn. We have seen this dictum carried beyond the classroom to engulf the entire school culture. The

---

LEARNING WINDOW 8.4
Stem Questions About How Important Significant
Contention Is to Promote Meaningful Change

✔ Why is it important to invite reflective dialogue?
✔ How can team learning be more productive at your school?
✔ What critical issues exist at your school which await your significant contention? The significant contention of your team?

premise is that only certain people should possess certain knowledge which, at their whim, they *may* dispose to others.

The invocation of team practice and team learning can stem the tide of a "limited scope" existence. When schoolpeople are asked to join to dialogue, invent, and reflect on their practices, they fill a void of time and space. Reflective practice causes people to envision beyond boundaries and challenge old assumptions. Individuals can become passionate practitioners for change in teaching and learning at the school when they authenticate the context of their daily work and chose to live a life of significant contention.

As we continue to search for answers about how to best reinvent our schools, it is important that we continue the dialogue. Dialogue among schoolpeople is the cornerstone of promoting change from within our own culture. The isolation of teachers, classified staff, and parents has been prolonged past the point of common sense. School leaders should make it a point to galvanize the independent intelligence that lives in the shareholder community so they will feel welcome to commit to collaborate in team learning.

It is only when people come together to honestly assess the "hows" and "whys" of enhancing productivity that quality education will become a reality. Every person wants to make a contribution. Work should offer the opportunity for self-growth. The possibilities of team learning presents intriguing hope for professional and personal development.

I sincerely hope this book has some impact on your understanding of team learning. There are many starting points for team learning in schools. It is most important that you initiate a plan of action as soon as possible to help move your organization forward. Once a plan is in place, you will establish priorities about what you can do to facilitate change. Change begins with individuals. Individuals can inspire others to embrace change. A great deal of learning transpires in dialogue sessions. A learning organization begins with a first conversation and grows one conversation at a time.

Team learning is both an intellectual and heartfelt opportunity to explore the human desire to labor at the edge of knowledge. It is evidence of the human mind's hunger to explore and share learning that will be the genesis of emerging self-discoveries in our schools. Those individuals who live a life of significant contention will be the ones who lead schools to new places in the heart and interesting landscapes of the mind.

As recently as five years ago, leaders in schools would not have seen a future in asking schoolpeople to join together in team learning enterprises to pursue quality ventures. Suddenly, remarkably, their vision has improved.

A life of significant contention awaits those who desire to imagine the possible. It is a cerebral quest, a courageous exploration of the soul. When we commit to work together to create new possibilities we forge a collective, visionary light. And the light that shines through is dazzling.

ENDNOTES

1. David Clark and Terry A. Astuto, "Redirecting Reform: Challenges to Popular Assumptions About Teachers and Students," *Phi Delta Kappan*, March 1994.
2. Harold Stevenson and James W. Stigler, *The Learning Gap* (New York: Summit Books, 1992).
3. Peter Senge, *The Fifth Discipline* (New York: Doubleday, 1990).
4. Douglas McGregor, *The Human Side of Enterprise* (New York: McGraw-Hill, 1960).
5. Everett A. Rogers, *Diffusion of Innovations* (New York: Free Press, 1982).
6. Ellen Meyers, "Changing Schools, Changing Roles—Redefining the Role of the Principal in a Restructured School" (New York: IMPACT II—The Teachers Network, William T. Grant Foundation, May 1995).
7. Bruce Joyce and Emily Calhoun, "School Renewal: An Inquiry, Not a Formula," *Educational Leadership*, April 1995.

LEARNING WINDOWS

8.1 Richard Farson, *Management of the Absurd: Paradoxes in Leadership* (New York: Simon & Schuster, 1996).
8.3 Price Pritchett and Ron Pound, *The Stress of Organizational Change* (Dallas, TX: Pritchett and Associates, 1996).

BIBLIOGRAPHY

Abbott, James E. "Extended Conversations." *The Total Quality Review*, November/December 1995.

———. "Guerilla Quality Management. *Education*, Summer Issue 1994.

———. *Managing at the Speed of Light: The ABC's of TQM for Schools.* Boston: American Press, 1998.

———. "Measuring Quality with Fuzzy Logic." *The TQM Magazine*, 8, No. 4 (September 1996).

———. "Sharing Craft Knowledge: The Soul of Principal Peer Assessment." *Technological Horizons in Education Journal*, November 1996.

———. "The Renaissance Principal: Leading the Movement to Transform Education." *The Executive Educator*, September 1994.

———. *The Restructuring of the Los Angeles Unified School District: When Dinosaurs Learned How to Dance.* Las Vegas: Q.M. Press, 1994.

Adams, Scott. *Dogbert's Top Secret Management Handbook.* New York: Harper Business, 1996.

Apodaca, Ted. "Programs Change Mundane Curriculum." *Gardena Valley News*, November 28, 1996.

Auel, Jean M. *The Mammoth Hunters.* New York: Bantam, 1991.

Barth, Roland. "A Personal Vision of a Good School." *Phi Delta Kappan*, March 1990.

———. *Improving Schools from Within: Teachers, Parents and Principals Can Make the Difference.* San Francisco: Jossey-Bass, 1991.

———. *Run School Run.* Cambridge, MA: Harvard University Press, 1980.

———. "You Can't Lead Where You Won't Go." In Anne Turnbaugh Lockwood, *Research and Schools: Selected Investigations on Education Reform.* Albany, NY: State University of New York Press, 1997.

Belasco, James. *Teaching the Elephant to Dance: The Manager's Guide to Empowering Change.* New York: Penguin, 1991.

Bennis, Warren, and Burt Nanus. *Leaders: The Strategies for Taking Charge.* New York: Harper and Row Publishers, 1985.

Bensimon, E.M., and A. Neuman. *Redesigning Collegiate Leadership: Teams and Teamwork in Higher Education.* Baltimore: Johns Hopkins University Press, 1993.

Bolman, Lee G. *Leading with Soul.* San Francisco: Jossey-Bass, 1996.

Cambor, Kathleen. *The Book of Mercy.* New York: Farrar, Straus and Giroux, 1996.

Castaneda, Carlos. *The Teachings of Don Juan: A Yaqui Way of Knowledge.* New York: Simon & Schuster (Pocket Books), 1968.

Clark, David, and Terry A. Astuto. "Redirecting Reform: Challenges to Popular Assumptions About Teachers and Students." *Phi Delta Kappan*, March 1994.

Deming, W. Edwards. *Out of the Crisis*. Cambridge, MA: M.I.T. Center for
Advanced Engineering Study, 1986.

Drucker, Peter. *Managing the Non-Profit Organization*. New York:
HarperCollins, 1990.

———. *The New Realities*. New York: Harper and Row, 1989.

Farson, Richard. *Management of the Absurd: Paradoxes in Leadership*. New York:
Simon & Schuster, 1996.

Garvin, David A. "Building a Learning Organization." *Harvard Business Review*,
July/August 1993.

Goleman, Daniel. *Emotional Intelligence*. New York: Bantam, 1995.

Huffington, Ariana. *The Fourth Instinct: The Call of the Soul*. New York:
Simon & Schuster, 1994.

Isaacs, William. "Dialogue: The Power of Collective Thinking." In Kellie
T. Wardman, ed. *Reflections on Creating Learning Organizations*, Cambridge,
MA: Pegasus Communications, 1994.

Ishikawa, Kaoru. *What Is Total Quality Control? The Japanese Way*. Translated
by David J. Lu. Englewood Cliffs, NJ: Prentice-Hall, 1985.

Joyce, Bruce, and Emily Calhoun. "School Renewal: An Inquiry, Not a
Formula." *Educational Leadership*, April 1995.

Katzenbach, Jon R., and Douglas K. Smith. *The Wisdom of Teams: Creating a
High Performance Organization*. Cambridge, MA: Harvard Business, 1993.

Kelley, Robert. *The Gold-Collar Worker: Harnessing the Brainpower of the New
Workforce*. Reading, MA: Addison-Wesley Publishing, 1985.

Kotter, John P. "Leading Change: Why Transformational Efforts Fail." *Harvard
Business Review*, March/April 1995.

Kundera, Milan. *Slowness*. Translated by Linda Asher. New York:
HarperCollins, 1994.

Latham, Gary, and Kenneth Wexley. *Increasing Productivity Through Performance
Appraisal*. Reading, MA: Addison-Wesley, 1981.

Lynch, Dudley, and Paul L. Kordis. *The Strategy of the Dolphin: Scoring a Win in
a Chaotic World*. New York: Fawcett Columbine, 1988.

Marshall, Catherine, J. Patterson, D. Rogers, and J. Steele. "Caring as a Career:
An Alternative Perspective for Educational Administration." *Educational
Administration Quarterly* 32, No. 2 (April 1996).

Maslow, Abraham. *Toward a Psychology of Being*. Princeton, NJ: D. Van
Nostrand, 1962.

May, Rollo. *The Courage to Create*. New York: W.W. Norton and Company, 1975.

McGregor, Douglas. *The Human Side of Enterprise*. New York: McGraw-Hill, 1960.

McKee, Bradford. "Turn Your Workers into a Team." *Nations Business*, July 1992.

Meyers, Ellen. "Changing Schools, Changing Roles—Redefining the Role of
the Principal in a Restructured School." New York: IMPACT II—The
Teachers Network, William T. Grant Foundation, May 1995.

Moller, Gayle, and Marilyn Katzenbach, eds. *Every Teacher a Leader: Realizing the Potential of Teacher Leadership.* San Francisco: Jossey-Bass, 1996.

Morehouse, Debra L. *Total Quality Management.* Shawnee Mission, KS: National Press Publications, 1992.

Noddings, N. *The Challenge to Care in Schools: An Alternative Approach to Education.* New York: Teachers College Press, 1992.

Nolan, Vincent. *The Innovator's Handbook: The Skills of Innovative Management.* New York: Penguin, 1989.

Ortese, Anna Maria. *The Music Behind the Wall: Selected Stories*, Volume I. Translated by Henry Martin. New York: McPherson and Company, 1995.

Pasmore, William A. *Creating Strategic Change: Designing the Flexible, High-Performing Organization.* New York: John Wiley and Sons, Inc., 1994.

Peters, Tom. *Thriving on Chaos: Handbook for a Management Revolution.* New York: Harper and Row, 1987.

Pirsig, Robert M. *Zen and the Art of Motorcycle Maintenance: An Inquiry into Values.* New York: Morrow and Company, 1974.

Prigogine, Ilya. "As a Scientist," *New Perspectives Quarterly*, Spring 1992.

Pritchett, Price, and Ron Pound. *The Stress of Organizational Change.* Dallas, TX: Pritchett and Associates, 1996.

Proust, Marcel. *Remembrance of Things Past.* New York: Random House, 1986.

Pryor, Fred. *The Energetic Manager.* Englewood Cliffs, NJ: Prentice-Hall, 1987.

Rogers, Everett A. *Diffusion of Innovations.* New York: Free Press, 1982.

Rosenholtz, S. *Teacher's Workplace: The Social Organization of Schools.* New York: Longman, 1989.

Schaps, Eric. "Pushing Back for the Center." *Education Week*, January 22, 1997.

Scholtes, Peter. *The Team Handbook: How to Use Teams to Improve Quality.* Madison, WI: Joiner and Associates, 1989.

Schon, Donald A. *The Reflective Practitioner: How Professionals Think in Action.* New York: Basic Books, 1983.

Senge, Peter. *The Fifth Discipline: The Art and Practice of the Learning Organization.* New York: Doubleday, 1990.

———. "The Leader's New Work: Building a Learning Organization." M.I.T. *Sloan Management Review*, Fall Issue 1990.

Solzhenitsyn, Alexander. *A World Split Apart.* New York: Harper and Row, 1978.

Stevenson, Harold, and James W. Stigler. *The Learning Gap.* New York: Summit Books, 1992.

Tuckman, Bruce. "Development Sequence in Small Groups." *Psychological Bulletin*, No. 1 (1955).

Torres, Cresencio. *The Tao of Teams.* San Diego: Pfeiffer and Company, 1994.

Walton, Mary. *The Deming Management Method.* New York: Perigree Books, 1986.

Wardman, Kellie, ed. *Reflections on Creating Learning Organizations.* Cambridge, MA: Pegasus Communications, 1994.

Watson, Charles. *Managing with Integrity: Insights from America's C.E.O.'s.*
New York: Praeger, 1991.

Weick, Karl. *The Social Psychology of Organizing.* Reading, MA: Addison-
Wesley Publishers, 1979.

Weisinger, Hendrie. *The Critical Edge.* New York: Harper and Row, 1989.

Wheatley, Margaret. *Leadership and the New Science: Learning About
Organization from an Orderly Universe.* San Francisco: Berrett-Koehler
Publishers, 1994.

INDEX

READER FEEDBACK
Fax to ASQ Quality Press Acquisitions: 414–272–1734

Comments and Areas for Improvement:
Quality Team Learning for Schools: A Principal's Perspective (Abbott H0973)

Please give us your comments, feedback, and suggestions for making this book more useful. We believe in the importance of continuous improvement and in meeting your needs. Your comments will help determine what improvements can be made in all ASQ Quality Press books.

Please share your opinion by circling the number below:

Ratings of the Book	Needs Work		Satisfactory		Excellent	Comments
Structure, flow, and logic	1	2	3	4	5	
Content, ideas, and information	1	2	3	4	5	
Style, clarity, ease of reading	1	2	3	4	5	
Held my interest	1	2	3	4	5	
Met my overall expectations	1	2	3	4	5	

I read the book because:

The best part of the book was:

The least satisfactory part of the book was:

Other suggestions for improvement:

General comments:

Thank you for your feedback. If you do not have access to a fax machine, please mail this form to: ASQ Quality Press, 611 East Wisconsin Avenue, P.O. Box 3005, Milwaukee, WI 53201-3005 Phone: 414-272-8575